VEGE with Schmecks Appeal

EDNA STAEBLER

McGRAW-HILL RYERSON
Montreal Toronto

McCLELLAND & STEWART
Toronto

Vegetables with Schmecks Appeal
© 1990 by Edna Staebler

First published in 1990 by

McGraw-Hill Ryerson Limited
330 Progress Avenue
Toronto, Canada
M1P 2Z5

McClelland & Stewart Limited
481 University Avenue
Suite 900
Toronto, Canada
M5G 2E9

ISBN 0-7710-8279-7

1 2 3 4 5 6 7 8 9 0   W   9 8 7 6 5 4 3 2 1 0

Printed and bound in Canada

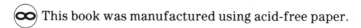 This book was manufactured using acid-free paper.

Canadian Cataloguing in Publication Data
Staebler, Edna, date
   Vegetables with schmecks appeal

(Schmecks appeal cookbook series)
ISBN 0-7710-8279-7

1. Cookery (Vegetables).   2. Cookery, Mennonite.
3. Cookery – Ontario – Waterloo (Regional
municipality).   I. Title.   II. Series: Staebler,
Edna, — date   Schmecks appeal cookbook series.

TX801.S84 1990   641.6'5   C90-095477-9

CONTENTS

INTRODUCTION   1

VEGETABLE COOKING HINTS   3

ASPARAGUS   4

BEANS   7

BEETS   13

BROCCOLI   14

BRUSSELS SPROUTS   17

CABBAGE   18

CARROTS   21

CAULIFLOWER   25

CELERY   26

CORN ON THE COB   27

CUCUMBERS   30

EGGPLANT   32

ENDIVE   34

FIDDLEHEADS   35

GARLIC   36

GREENS   38

JERUSALEM ARTICHOKES   41

KOHLRABI   42

LEEKS   43

MUSHROOMS   44

ONIONS   46

PARSNIPS   49

PEAS   50

PEPPERS   51

POTATOES 53

PUMPKIN 64

SALSIFY 65

SAUERKRAUT 66

SQUASH 68

TOMATOES 70

TURNIPS 74

ZUCCHINI 76

MIXED VEGETABLES 79

SAUCES FOR VEGETABLES 84

INDEX 90

INTRODUCTION

There isn't a Mennonite farm that hasn't a garden near its sprawling farmhouse. As soon as the well-manured ground in Bevvy's garden has been cultivated in spring, she plants seeds in long, neat rows; then she looks out her kitchen window to watch the vegetables grow. "Quick, Salome," she'll call on a sunny June morning. "I think the beans came up last night." And out they'll both run to rejoice at the promise of coming abundance. Every day they keep watching, comparing growth with neighbours and friends. "My beets are slow this year," one will say; or, "I don't think my cauliflower will amount to much," or, "There's going to be a bumper crop of peas."

All Waterloo County benefits from the Mennonites' love of their land and what it produces. Nowhere else in the world that I've seen can vegetables be purchased in such variety, profusion, and excellence. The farmers' markets on Saturday (and on Wednesday in summer and fall) are crowded with people buying baskets and baskets of vegetables that a few hours earlier were sparkling with dew.

Yet one day my sister Norm said to me, "Vegetables are a necessary nuisance, aren't they? Ever notice when you go out for dinner you remember the meat, the dessert, and maybe the soup or the salad? You seldom remember the vegetables."

And even Bevvy has said, "Vegetables are always extra good in summer when I can fetch them from the garden and put them right in the boiling water, fresh and sweet, but in winter they have to be kind of doctored up a little to give them some taste—except, of course, sauerkraut."

There are no directions for preparing vegetables for dinner or supper in the little handwritten black notebook in which Bevvy has copied, swapped, and inherited recipes. "Ach, I've cooked so many vegetables already I just put in what I think would make them go down good. Like for most things, I tell by the feel or the taste. Since I was a little girl I helped my mam and I learned from her just like

1

my girls learn from me. That's why it's hard to give the amounts of a recipe to a stranger."

Using the vague instructions Bevvy has given me, I've tried to write definite measurements and methods. Forgive me, please, if you find some of the directions inadequate. If you test and taste for yourself you might achieve something fantastic; anyway, you'll have fun and a feeling of enthusiatic adventure—integral components of Waterloo County cookery, which is a heritage from the Mennonite pioneers who in 1800 came here in their Conestoga wagons from Pennsylvania and devised palatable ways to cook whatever they found in the wilderness or could grow on the land they were clearing.

For every vegetable and fruit grown in Canada there is a season. And when that season comes, I go to the farmers' markets and indulge—perhaps overindulge—in whatever comes along. In the spring I can hardly wait for asparagus, dandelion greens, rhubarb, then strawberries and peas. The growing time for peas and asparagus is so short I eat them—raw or cooked—every day.

Throughout the summer there are so many vegetables to choose from: I bring home baskets of green and yellow wax beans, broccoli, corn, tomatoes, eggplant, cucumber, kohlrabi, spinach, greens, fresh herbs, salsify, and zucchini.

In the fall I buy cabbage, carrots, beets, parsnips, squash, onions, potatoes: I store them in my cold guest room and use them throughout the winter, along with the summer vegetables I have tucked into my freezer, and the tinned vegetables in my hall cupboard. I don't have hundreds of jars on shelves in a basement as the Old Order Mennonites do. But I have enough to give me assurance that I won't starve if the half-mile lane to my cottage is covered with ice for days or weeks at a time or winds from the north or east are blowing and the snow is drifting.

I try not to let a day of my life pass without eating vegetables. Many can be eaten raw, with no more preparation than slicing, peeling, and dipping. Soups and Salads with Schmecks Appeal *(in this cookbook series)* gives much inspiration; so should Lunches, Suppers and

Brunches *and* Sweets, Sours and Drinks. *In this book, most of the recipes are for vegetable side dishes to be eaten on a plate with a main course or as a vegetarian meal. All are easy to prepare and tasty. They should keep you healthy, happy, and wise.*

VEGETABLE COOKING HINTS

Prepare vegetables just before it's time to cook them—don't drown their vitamins by soaking them in water.

• Don't thaw frozen vegetables before cooking.

• Cook vegetables in their skins as often as possible to retain vitamins.

• Bring to a boil quickly then turn down heat to finish cooking.

• Cook till just crisp-tender, except potatoes, turnip, and squash.

• Cooking time depends on size and age of vegetable. Don't watch a half-hour TV program as a timer. Pay attention.

• Prick for doneness with an ice pick.

• Save vegetable cooking water for sauces, gravy, soups, and drinks.

• Serve as soon as cooked.

Buttered vegetables—1 to 3 tablespoons butter to 2 cups vegetables

Creamed vegetables—1 cup sauce to 2 cups vegetables.

All the very old cookbooks tell us to cook vegetables for hours and hours. I'm surprised that our ancestors survived to produce us!

The number of servings I've suggested in these recipes is approximate: more or less ¾ of a cupful per person—not nearly enough for a growing boy but too much for a little old grandma. You can figure out how much you'll need by adding up the number of cupfuls in the recipe. But remember that some things swell and others shrink. Bevvy says, "How much you make depends on how many people you cook for. We don't like to run short on anything but we don't like to waste nothing neither."

ASPARAGUS

*During our all-too-short asparagus season I heard a friend
say, "Oh, I'm sick of asparagus, I've been buying it almost
every week since January."*

For me those were fighting words!

*When I see asparagus in the supermarkets in winter I am
often tempted to buy it because I like it so much, and
spring seems far away. But I always resist the temptation
because I have an obsession about buying foods grown in
our own country. I'm afraid if we buy imported vegetables
there soon won't be any Canadian-grown foods. Or any
Canadian farmers who love and nurture our land like
Bevvy Martin and Hannah and Eva.*

*Whenever I go to Eva's place in the spring she'll say,
"Joanna (or Julia or Florence), go out in the garden and
get Edna some asparagus," and soon the girls will come
back with a great bundle for me to take home.*

*What can I do with so much just for me? I keep out
enough for an immediate meal of nothing-else-but, then I
wrap the rest in a wet tea towel, slide it into a plastic bag
and put it in the crisper in my fridge, where it would keep
very well for a week or two if I didn't enjoy some every
day until time for replenishment from Eva.*

*Sometimes I freeze asparagus: I clean it thoroughly,
plunge it into boiling water for 2 or 3 minutes, wrap it in
plastic, and store it in my freezer to use in the winter. Not
as good as fresh asparagus, but at least a reminder of
spring.*

SPRINGTIME ASPARAGUS

I stand my asparagus stalks, cut end down, in salted water and
steam them for about 7 minutes until just tender.

I like asparagus so much simply with butter melted over it
that I never try anything fancy except occasionally—to stretch
it—I make a cream or mild cheese sauce on toast.

Never throw away the water your asparagus was cooked in;
keep it in the fridge to use in soups or with a bouillon cube

melted in it and served hot in a mug, or mix it with tomato juice or V-8 for a cold or hot drink. It's full of vitamins and flavour.

BEVVY'S ASPARAGUS CASSEROLE

On a cold winter's day when you're dreaming of May, get out a bundle of **frozen asparagus**. Don't thaw it—put it into a buttered casserole, sprinkle it with **salt and pepper**, and pour over it 1 cup **sour cream**. Spread over it a cupful of **breadcrumbs** that have been mixed with ¼ cup **melted butter**. Bake at 350°F until the asparagus is soft and the crumbs are golden—about 45 minutes.

FRENCH ASPARAGUS

The first time I visited my friend Françoise, she was young, beautiful, unmarried, and still living near Arrass, north of Paris, in the chateau that has belonged to her family since 1668.

Every day for dinner in the banquet-size dining room, the first course was uniformly small, bleached white asparagus, which Françoise daintily dipped into melted butter with her fingers. She told me it was grown in the chateau's garden and covered with a mound of earth to cut off the sun and keep the stalks white and the flavour mild.

When I was in Alsace, asparagus in a restaurant was served the same way, with paper-thin slices of smoked red ham and crusty French bread.

Though I enjoyed the delicacy of French asparagus, I prefer Canada's more robust green variety, which shoots from the fertile soil into the sunlight.

ASPARAGUS FROMAGE

For a light luncheon, this is a breath of spring. Serve it with herbed biscuits.

> **1 cup mushrooms, whole or sliced**
> **2 tablespoons butter**
> **2 tablespoons flour**
> **1 cup milk**
> **½ teaspoon salt**
> **Pinch dry mustard**
> **2 tablespoons sherry**
> **2 bunches asparagus (about 2 pounds)**
> **½ cup toasted almonds or sunflower seeds**
> **¼ cup grated Cheddar cheese**

Sauté the mushrooms in butter over low heat. Remove the mushrooms; blend the flour into remaining butter in skillet; stir in the milk gradually. Cook until the sauce is thickened, stirring constantly. Add salt, mustard, and sherry. Steam or boil the asparagus, drain, then arrange on a flat ovenproof serving pan. Cover with the almonds and mushrooms. Pour sauce over all. Sprinkle with cheese and broil 5 to 6 inches from source of heat until cheese is melted.

BEANS

*In July and August, the Kitchener and Waterloo farmers'
markets are flooded with millions of beans: slim, crisp,
bright green and yellow wax beans, fat pole beans, lima
beans, baskets so full they flow over.*

*I buy beans every week and squeeze them into the
overloaded crisper in my fridge. Beans are good served
with any kind of meat—or without—and so easy to
prepare.*

*Rinse in cold water, then snap or cut off the stem end,
and the beans are ready to be boiled or steamed for about
7 minutes. Season with butter, salt, and lots of pepper.
Pass them around the table; there won't be a bean left over.*

*If you've kept fresh beans in your fridge a few days and
they seem to have lost their bloom—or if you use frozen
beans—you might pep them up by adding some herbs to
the cooking water: oregano, basil, thyme, or tarragon will
do. Or use a bouquet garni (page 86).*

*Add a chopped onion or a tablespoon or two of onion
soup mix. Just before serving, you might pour over the
beans a cheese or white sauce, or heated sour cream with
snippets of chives, dill, or parsley.*

*Over hot, buttered beans you might sprinkle sautéed
mushrooms, chopped toasted almonds or walnuts, or crisp
bacon bits.*

*Think of more things and try them. Beans are a
wonderful source for creative, enjoyable cooking—and
eating.*

SWISS BEAN OR CARROT CASSEROLE

This is one of my absolute favourites. I make it often and have to hand out the recipe every time.

1 pound fresh (or 2 packages frozen) French-cut green beans (or cut beans in 1-inch pieces) or sliced carrots
4 tablespoons butter
1 teaspoon sugar
2 tablespoons flour
1 onion, finely chopped
Salt and pepper
1 cup sour cream
⅔ cup dry breadcrumbs or Rice Krispies or corn flakes for topping
1 cup grated Cheddar cheese

Cook the beans or carrots until just soft. Melt 2 tablespoons of the butter and stir in sugar, flour, onion, salt, and pepper. Stir in the sour cream and heat but don't boil. Fold in the cooked beans or carrots and put all into a buttered casserole. For topping, melt remaining butter and mix with breadcrumbs—or what have you—and sprinkle over the casserole. Then sprinkle the grated cheese over all. Bake at 400°F for 20 minutes—just long enough to heat through and have the top golden.

SCHNIPPLED BEAN SALAD

This most popular Waterloo County specialty is both salad and vegetable. It is served on the plate with the main course—not as a separate salad. Whenever the Berton family comes to my house for a weekend, I must make bean salad because they all like it so well. How many beans to use is a problem because people always eat more than they think they can; I remember when Ralph Allen, Pierre Berton, Ian Sclanders—all *Maclean's* editors—and their wives came for Sunday dinner. I used six quarts of fresh yellow beans for the salad, and there was just a small dish left.

1 quart green or yellow string beans
1 onion, sliced
1 teaspoon salt

Dressing:

1 teaspoon sugar
¼ teaspoon pepper
1 teaspoon vinegar
½ cup sour cream

Cut the stems off the beans, wash them, then schnippel them. That means cutting the beans on a slant in very thin slices, each bean cut into 3 or 4 long slices. (Or you could use frozen French-cut beans—but they're not as good.) Put the beans into boiling water and cook them just long enough to be soft. Drain and cool. Meantime, peel and slice the onion, sprinkle it liberally with salt, and stir it around, then let it stand at least 15 minutes, giving it a stir now and then. In a bowl large enough to contain the beans, blend the dressing ingredients.

Take the salted onion into your hand, and with the other hand squeeze as much of the juice out of the onion as you can. Put the squeezed onion into the dressing (the juice, too, if you like). Pour the well-drained beans into the dressing and mix till all the beans are coated. You might need more cream.

HANNAH'S HANDY CANNED BEAN RECIPE

Hannah kept telling me about this easy, tasty way of serving canned green beans. "We make it often," she said. "We really like it. And it's so handy and easy to make when somebody drops in."

2 tablespoons butter or margarine
1 cup breadcrumbs
½ teaspoon paprika
¼ cup grated cheese
1 quart canned green beans, with the liquid
1 tablespoon oil
½ teaspoon garlic salt

Prepare topping: melt butter in skillet, add breadcrumbs, and stir over medium heat until crumbs are golden in colour. Blend

in paprika and cheese. Remove from heat and mix well. Heat the
beans and drain off liquid. Add oil and garlic salt, toss lightly,
top with crumb mixture, and serve.

MAGDALINA HORST'S SCHNITZEL BEANS

In Magdalina's old, old recipe the beans are supposed to be
cooked for an hour, the tomatoes added and cooked for 2 hours
longer. It can all be done in half an hour or less in these vitamin-
saving times.

3 slices bacon, cut in narrow strips
1½ pounds green beans, cut in 1-inch pieces
3 large onions, sliced
1 teaspoon salt
¼ teaspoon pepper
1 cup hot water
4 medium tomatoes, cut in pieces

Fry the bacon until crisp, remove it but leave a tablespoon of
the fat in the pan. Mix in the beans, onions, salt, pepper, and hot
water, and cook till the beans are almost tender before putting
in the tomatoes and cooking until they are soft. Serve with
crumbled bacon on top. This is a very good, savoury dish.

DRIED BEANS

The most practical of winter vegetables: rich in protein—almost a meat substitute—low in cholesterol, inexpensive, and
they'll keep for months in a tin that takes little space in the back
of your cupboard. There are many varieties, fairly interchangeable. Red kidney beans are used in chili, flat green limas in
cream. Most useful and popular are the little white navy beans
that are so tasty baked with molasses, tomatoes, a ham bone,
and perhaps a tot of rum.

A pound of dried beans should make 6 cupfuls when cooked.

Dried beans should be soaked in cold water overnight, but if
you forget to do that you can speed up the process. Put them in
cold water on the stove, bring them to a boil, and boil for a few
minutes, then let them stand in the water for an hour or more.
Use the soaking water for cooking; beans must be simmered a

very long time, then baked in the oven till their delicious aroma makes you impatient to get at them. Be sure to make a big potful because they reheat and freeze well. You'll be glad to have a repeat before the winter is over.

BAKED BEANS

Wonderful if you want to feed a lot of young people who are going skating or skiing—or the older folks who are just going out for a walk.

4 cups little white beans
½ cup molasses
2 teaspoons mustard
½ teaspoon pepper
½ cup ketchup
2½ quarts water, or liquid in which beans were boiled
½ pound salt pork, cut into pieces

Soak the beans overnight. In the soaking water, cook them slowly till the skins burst. Drain and save the liquid. Mix molasses, mustard, pepper, ketchup and 2 cups of liquid from the beans. Put one piece of pork in the bottom of a bean pot or baking dish, add the beans and put the rest of the pork on top. Pour molasses mixture over beans and add enough bean liquid to cover. Bake, covered, for 5 hours at 300°F, adding more liquid during the baking as the beans become dry. Take off the lid for the last half-hour of baking. The beans should be brown and rich, moist and abundant. Remember beans swell, but don't be afraid to cook plenty of them; they're just as good heated over.

CARIBBEAN BAKED BEANS

My little Save the Children foster child in Jamaica sent me a handmade cookbook that had a few recipes I could use. This one was easy to adapt to our ways.

Follow the recipe for baked beans. Add a sliced **onion**, and instead of the ketchup stir in ¼ cup **dark rum**. (And don't empty the bottle while you're waiting for the beans to bake.)

LIMA BEANS WITH CREAM

Fresh limas are best, but if you can't get them you might soak dried limas overnight in cold water, drain them and proceed:

**3 cups limas, fresh or soaked
Salt
3 cups water
6 slices bacon
2 tablespoons flour
1½ cups water in which limas cooked
¼ cup cream or ½ cup whole milk**

Cook the beans in salted water till they are tender. Drain and save 1½ cups of the water. Cut the bacon into ½-inch bits and fry till crisp; remove from the pan, pour out all but 2 table-spoons of the fat. Blend the flour with the bacon fat in the pan and slowly add the hot water from the limas, stirring until it thickens, then pour in cream or milk. Add the limas and bacon bits, and simmer a few minutes before serving.

HERBED AND BUTTERED LIMAS

Cook the limas in salted water till soft, drain and blend in butter and herbs. Serve hot.

Red kidney beans can be used in the same way as limas but are most often used in chili con carne with meat to make a whole meal.

Anemic canned beans can be made flavourful if you pep them up with one tablespoon brown sugar, one or two tablespoons molasses, and a tablespoon or two of ketchup. Let them simmer for a few minutes. Of course, they can't be compared with the real home-baked beans, but the doctoring does make them edible—and it's fast.

BEETS

If you are lucky enough to have little beets fresh from a garden, boil them quickly till they are tender, skin them, drop them into hot melted butter, sprinkle them with salt and pepper and be happy.

To prepare beets, cut off the leaves (cook them like spinach if they are fresh), leaving a 1-inch stem and the tail root to preserve the colour. Young beets will cook in about 20 minutes; old, larger beets take much longer unless you use a pressure cooker. When beets are tender drain off the water, blanch them with cold water but don't let them stand in it; slip the skins from the beets before they are cold. Old beets are best when finely chopped, sprinkled with sugar, salt, pepper, and plenty of butter.

SUESS UND SAUER ROTE RIEVE
(Sweet and Sour Beets)

This Pennsylvania Dutch recipe went to Harvard.

½ **cup sugar**
1 **teaspoon salt**
1 **tablespoon cornstarch**
¼ **cup vinegar or red wine**
½ **cup water**
3 **cups beets, cooked, then sliced or diced**
2 **tablespoons butter**

Mix the sugar, salt, cornstarch, and stir as you add the vinegar and water. Cook the mixture 5 minutes, or till it thickens a bit; add the beets and let stand half an hour. Before serving, heat to boiling point and stir in the butter.

BROCCOLI

I hate to say this but it is safer to soak broccoli in salted water for a while so worms may come out and float on top. Remove any discoloured parts and part of the stem. Cook whole, or broken into flowerets. Boil for 15 to 20 minutes—don't let it get too soft or it's horrid. Serve with melted butter, cheese, brown sauce, and buttered crumbs.

LEMON DRESSING FOR BROCCOLI

"Let stand several hours for these diversities to get together in one grand mysterious flavour." That's what a very old cookbook says. So easy and so good—hot or cold.

¼ cup lemon juice
¼ cup oil
1 clove garlic, crushed
1 tablespoon finely chopped onion
1 teaspoon sugar
½ teaspoon salt
¼ teaspoon paprika

Blend all ingredients and let stand for several hours. Shake well, heat, and pour over hot cooked broccoli. You might try it with cauliflower, too.

SNOW-CAPPED BROCCOLI

Anything my sister Norm makes or likes is guaranteed to be good. This recipe of hers is a nice way to serve company.

1 bunch broccoli
1 tablespoon melted butter
2 eggs, separated
¼ teaspoon salt

¹⁄₂ **cup mayonnaise**
½ **cup grated cheese**

Cook broccoli. Arrange stem ends to centre of a pie plate and brush with butter. In a bowl beat egg whites and salt until stiff. Gently fold the egg yolks, mixed with mayonnaise, into the egg whites. Spoon mixture in the centre of broccoli and sprinkle grated cheese on top. Bake at 350°F for 12 to 15 minutes.

BROCCOLI CASSEROLE

You could make a meal of this. And it's easy to prepare.

1 stalk or 2 packages frozen broccoli
2½ cups crushed crackers
2 tablespoons butter, melted
⅓ cup mayonnaise
1 can cream of mushroom soup
3 tablespoons minced onion
1 cup grated cheese

Cook the broccoli until tender. Drain. Stir the cracker crumbs into the melted butter. Spread half the cracker crumbs over the bottom of a well-buttered 9 inch x 9 inch baking pan. Place the broccoli evenly in the pan. Stir together mayonnaise, mushroom soup, onion, and half the cheese. Pour evenly over the broccoli. Sprinkle with remaining cracker crumbs and cheese. Bake in a 350°F oven for about one hour.

SHORT-CUT BROCCOLI DIVAN (WITH OR WITHOUT CHICKEN)

When I was writing *More Food That Really Schmecks*, Martina Schneicker sent me this recipe from Goderich; she said it was wonderful. Nine years later Kit came to my house from Brantford and told me about a great way to serve broccoli. Her recipe was the same as Martina's but she used cream of mushroom soup instead of chicken soup. She didn't use chicken, either.

6 chicken breasts
1 bunch broccoli
2 cans cream of chicken or mushroom soup
1 cup mayonnaise
1 teaspoon lemon juice
½ teaspoon curry powder
½ cup grated Cheddar cheese
¼ cup butter
1 cup breadcrumbs

Boil the chicken until tender. Cook the broccoli till almost tender. Arrange chicken and broccoli in a flat baking dish. Blend the soup, mayonnaise, lemon juice, and curry, and pour it over the chicken and broccoli. Top with the cheese and buttered breadcrumbs. Bake at 350°F for 30 minutes.

BRUSSELS SPROUTS

Buy them on the stalk if you can and pick them off as you use them; they'll keep longer.

After cleaning the sprouts, steam or put them in boiling water for 8 to 10 minutes, take them out of the water, drain well, then warm them in butter. Shake the pan over low heat, covered, to keep them from sticking. Never, never overcook them. You could make a Béchamel sauce for them or a Mornay. In other words, a white sauce or cheese sauce. Then you might sprinkle them with a few crisply fried bacon bits or chopped toasted nuts.

SAVOURY SPROUTS

Easy. Put a quart of cooked sprouts in a casserole blended with a tin of tomato soup or tomato sauce. Sprinkle grated cheese over top and bake at 350°F for about 20 minutes, or until the cheese is toasty and the whole dish is hot.

You might try some of the broccoli recipes with sprouts.

CABBAGE

Never be without a cabbage in your house; you can do so many things with a cabbage. The fresher and greener it is the better, but even if you've had it around for a while and its outer leaves look a bit dingy, there's nothing wrong with the rest of it. You can use it in salads, in soup, in a casserole, or as a vegetable with meat and potatoes. It used to be inexpensive.

In the fall I buy the biggest, heaviest cabbage I can find at the market, put it in a plastic bag, and keep it in my cold storage room till it's small enough to put in my fridge. Every week I carefully take off a few of the outer leaves to make coleslaw, or hot slaw, or to shred and keep for several days in an airtight container in my fridge so I can easily mix as much as I want with salad dressing or other salad ingredients. One cabbage will last for months.

A doctor once told me that raw cabbage eaten every day would keep me vigorous: it's a rich source of vitamins A, B, and C, chlorine, calcium, sodium, and iron.

Red cabbage can be used in the same way as green cabbage; it is often preferable because its colour is attractive on a plate.

MOTHER'S HOT SLAW

This is wonderful; I eat it and enjoy it almost every single week during the winter. It is so easy and so good for me. It's great with potatoes and farmer's sausage, pork chops or ham when I have a visitor, but when I'm alone I make a whole meal of it without anything else—except dessert.

For one alone: Put about 1 tablespoon **butter** in the bottom of a heavy pot at moderate to low heat, let it melt, then drop in 1 sliced onion (optional) and 4 leaves of **cabbage**, cut into ¼-inch slices and always across the spines. Put the lid on the pot, set your timer for 15 or 20 minutes so you won't forget the cabbage while you read the evening paper. It wouldn't hurt to get up once or twice to give the pot a stir. Meantime, in a cup put 1 teaspoon **sugar**, ½ teaspoon **salt**, a good shake of **pepper**, and 2 teaspoons **vinegar**. Blend in 2 or 3 tablespoons **sour cream**. When the cabbage is crisply soft, stir in the sour cream mixture. Serve hot.

If you make this for more people, simply double or quadruple the amounts. I'm telling you, it really is special. Because she liked it so well, Janet Berton, a gourmet cook, asked me to make it three times during a week she was staying with me.

CABBAGE CHEESE

A whole meal can be made in minutes by slicing **cabbage leaves** about ¼ inch wide and placing them in a heavy pot with a tablespoon of **butter** melted on the bottom. Cover and cook over low heat until the cabbage is almost soft then stir in ½ cup grated **cheese**, cover and let stand until cheese melts. A perfect meal—protein and vegetable. Double it for two.

But if you want to serve four or more you might find it better to make this casserole in the oven.

3 tablespoons butter
3 tablespoons flour
1 cup grated Cheddar cheese
Salt
1 cup milk
1 head cabbage, about 2½ pounds, sliced
⅔ cup buttered breadcrumbs

Melt the butter. Stir in the flour, cheese, salt, and milk, stirring until the cheese melts. Put a third of the cabbage in a casserole, pour in a third of the cheese sauce, then repeat layers. Cover with buttered breadcrumbs and bake at 350°F until the cabbage is as soft as you like it. Not mushy.

CHINESE CABBAGE

Shred the cabbage, then boil or sauté 4 or 5 minutes. No longer. It's good with a cream or cheese sauce. It has a milder flavour than regular cabbage and can be used in the same recipes, as well as in salads.

BUBBLE AND SQUEAK

Another good way to use an aging cabbage: quick, easy, and tasty. But my friend Kath told me that in Devon Bubble and Squeak is just a fry-up of leftovers.

Cabbage, as much as you think you need (it shrinks)
1 potato per person
Some onion if you like
1 tablespoon bacon fat
1 tablespoon butter
¼ to ½ cup boiling water
Salt and pepper

Slice or chop the cabbage, and peel and slice the potato and onion. Melt the fat and butter in a large frying pan, then add the vegetables and boiling water. Season with salt and pepper, cover the pan with a tight lid, and cook over low heat until the potatoes are soft, about 15 minutes if you're single, longer if your frying pan is loaded. Stir the mixture occasionally and add more fat if necessary. If you'd like to brown it on the bottom, take off the lid after the potatoes are soft and let it develop a brown crust. This makes a good meal with cold meat or sausages and a salad or relish.

HANNAH'S RED CABBAGE

This is especially good with country pork sausage.

1 tablespoon butter
1 onion, chopped very fine
1 small red cabbage, shredded
1 cooking apple, chopped fine
4 teaspoons corn syrup
¼ cup lemon juice
1 tablespoon vinegar

Melt the butter and sauté the onion till soft. Add cabbage and apple, then add remaining ingredients and simmer, covered, for 30 minutes. Add more corn syrup if you want it sweeter.

CARROTS

No vegetable is used so often as the commonplace, colourful carrot, from the time it is tender and sweet and fresh from the garden till it is limp and tired after spending the winter packed in leaves in a cool cellar. Young carrots need no embellishment: the sweet, delicate flavour of the vegetable eaten raw or cooked for a few minutes in salted water is all that is necessary—with a bit of butter added before serving. But as time goes on and the carrot grows older, it may need some ingenuity to make it delectable. Never, never cut carrots into chunks, they look as if nobody cared.

CARROTS AND ONIONS

Not a bad winter vegetable dish when you have meat without any gravy.

6 carrots
6 onions
1 can mushroom soup
1 tablespoon chopped parsley
¼ teaspoon paprika
Toasted slivered almonds or sunflower seeds

Scrape the carrots, cut them in half lengthwise, then cut into 2-inch pieces. Peel and slice the onions and put in pan with carrots and enough water to cover. Simmer, covered, until tender; drain well, keeping ½ cup cooking water. Stir in the mushroom soup, the ½ cup reserved liquid, parsley, and paprika; heat through, stirring occasionally. Garnish with nuts or seeds.

BAKED CARROTS

This has a nutty, tangy flavour that amazes me.

Shred enough **raw carrots** to make 3 cups—about 6 large carrots; the shredder should have holes about ¼-inch in diameter. Put the carrots in a well-greased baking dish that can be used for serving. Sprinkle ½ teaspoon **salt**, ½ teaspoon **ginger** and ¼ teaspoon **pepper** over them; then pour on ½ cup **water** and mix well. Bake uncovered in a moderate oven for 45 minutes.

To make an easy, economical meal, arrange a pound of sausages or frankfurters on top of the carrots. Bake potatoes in the oven at the same time, and that's it.

CARROT CASSEROLE

Ruby says this is good as part of an oven meal. There's nothing to do at the last minute except bring it to the table.

2 cups carrots
½ cup mayonnaise
¼ cup finely chopped onion
¼ cup horseradish
2 tablespoons butter
⅔ cup breadcrumbs

Peel carrots and cut into 2-inch pieces. Cook in boiling water until almost tender. Drain, reserving ⅓ cup cooking liquid. Stir together mayonnaise, onion, horseradish, and reserved cooking liquid. Melt the butter. Stir in breadcrumbs. Place carrots in buttered casserole; pour sauce over carrots, then top with buttered breadcrumbs. Bake at 350°F for 20 minutes, or until top is brown.

GLAZED CARROTS

Carrots in winter are always more acceptable if you dress them up a bit—as Ruby does.

2 cups carrots, diced or sliced
2 tablespoons brown sugar
2 tablespoons butter
½ teaspoon salt
1 tablespoon lemon juice
¼ cup chopped fresh parsley, mint, or basil—or
**   whatever herb you prefer**

Cook the carrots in water until almost tender. Drain, put pan back on medium heat, adding sugar, butter, and salt. Shake the carrots until the butter and sugar have melted and the carrots turn golden. Stir in the lemon juice and sprinkle with chopped parsley or herbs.

CARROT LOAF

From four recipes for carrot loaf I developed this one. It has a
crunchy texture and is full of vitamins and flavour. If you are
a loner, you will probably make this a whole meal. If not you
might serve it with cold meat or hot meat, gravy, and potatoes.

1 onion, minced
2 tablespoons butter—3 if you're thin
6 or 7 carrots, grated—about 4 cups after grating
½ cup grated Cheddar cheese
½ cup finely sliced celery
2 eggs, lightly beaten
1 cup milk
1 cup breadcrumbs
1 teaspoon oregano or any herb you prefer
1 teaspoon salt
Pepper

Simmer the onion in the butter for a few minutes. In a bowl, mix
the carrots, cheese, and celery. Add the onion, eggs, milk,
breadcrumbs, herbs, and seasonings. Pack all into a loaf pan
and bake at 350°F for about 45 minutes.

TIRED CARROTS

Toward the end of the winter when carrots are limp—and I am,
too—I sometimes give them a shot by sprinkling them with any
of a variety of things in my herb cupboard: a tiny bit of **sage**,
summer savory, a dash of any of the **savoury salts**. Sometimes
I'll cut up an **onion** or two or a couple of sprigs or leaves of
celery or **parsley**. A cream sauce or brown sauce over carrots
is good with some meats. Best of all I'll sprinkle a tablespoon or
two of **sherry** or **lemon juice** over the carrots before serving.
And always I use plenty of butter and pepper.

   Nothing depresses me more than the constant sight of car-
rots-and-peas on every main dish in restaurants, hotel dining
rooms, and at banquets. There they inevitably are, a dull, dry
pile of flavourless orange and green. I won't have the combination in my house.

FOR VEGETARIANS

While earning her way through university, my nephew's ex-wife, Nancy, spent several summers working in a meat-packing plant. In her last year there she had to eviscerate chickens whose bodies were still warm and twitching. She'd come home at night, tired and unable to eat a good chicken dinner. Soon Nancy felt the same aversion to other meats. Eventually, travels in remote areas of the world, changing values, and a high regard for all life brought her to the conviction that vegetarianism was the only way for her and Jim.

People who are vegetarians seem to spend far more time—and perhaps more money—on food than people who eat meat. They must be sure they are getting enough protein from other sources, and they have to know all about where the vitamins are and how many they are getting every day.

They can't afford to be careless; what is more important than a healthy body and a lively mind? Nancy spent much time reading books on nutrition, shopping around for the right foods, and preparing them correctly. Every Saturday morning she'd go to the farmers' market and come home with baskets of fruits and vegetables.

When Nancy was cooking, the smell of onions, garlic, and "veggies," as she called them, was as tantalizing as any meat dinner that I might prepare. She had several vegetarian cookbooks but mainly relied on her own inventiveness. She concocted some interesting recipes, baked fruity muffins and crunchy cookies crammed with roughage and goodness. She ate great quantities of soy beans, cheese, nuts, whole grains. For a meal, she alone consumed a bowlful of green salad that I would put on the table for four or five people.

Nancy was always healthy. She swam to the end of the lake and back every day, went on long, vigorous canoe trips, skied and skated in the winter. She greatly influenced our family; we often have vegetarian meals. I feel guilty if I wear my beaver coat or mink stole—though the poor creatures have been dead a very long time. I would never buy another piece of fur or step on a caterpillar. But I still enjoy eating meat.

Inconsistent? Of course. So was Nancy—she wore leather sandals.

CAULIFLOWER

Cauliflower has so much flavour of its own it doesn't need much enhancement.

Break into flowerets and steam or boil in salted water with a bit of lemon juice to keep the vegetable white. Boil about 10 to 15 minutes, till barely tender; the worst sin is overcooking and serving soggy, grey, water-logged cauliflower. Drain it the moment it's tender and serve it at once with melted butter, buttered crumbs, a white sauce, or cheese sauce. Half white sauce and half mayonnaise blended together gives it a piquant flavour.

Raw cauliflower flowerets, whole or sliced, are most acceptable on a tray with other vegetable crudités and a dip.

Try broccoli recipes with cauliflower; the two vegetables belong to the same family and should be compatible.

CELERY

I don't know if it's true, but "they" used to say that celery is good for the nerves. Anyway, it tastes good fresh, raw, and crisp in slim slices, with a dip, or in salads. It gives flavour to other vegetables in soups, relishes, and casseroles but can be served as a vegetable in its own right.

Clean it with a brush because sand sticks between its strings—you might have to pull them off if they are inclined to be tough.

Slice celery and cook it in boiling, salted water, or water to which you have added a bouillon cube, a bit of onion soup mix, meat broth, consommé, or a sliced onion. When the celery is crisp-soft, you might cover it with browned butter, cream or cheese sauce, sour cream, mayonnaise, hollandaise, buttered crumbs, or chopped toasted nuts. Bevvy would serve it creamed on toast.

CELERIAC

This weird-looking root tastes like mild celery and can be sliced and eaten raw, with a dip or in salads, or pared, cooked, and served just as one would celery.

CORN ON THE COB

*You don't know how delicious corn can be until you taste it
fresh off the stalk. I used to phone the farmer's wife on the
next concession road to pick me some corn; I'd put a big
kettle of water on the stove, paddle down the lake in my
canoe to get the corn, husk it, and pop it into the boiling
salted water. As soon as the water returned to the boil, I'd
turn it off, let the corn stay in the water exactly 5 minutes,
then fish it out and eat it, slathered with butter, sprinkled
with pepper and salt. And that's all I'd want for supper,
thank you—except a fresh, sliced tomato.*

*If you know a farmer with corn in his garden, start
wooing him now. Beg him to call you when the corn ripens,
go fetch it, and cook it the minute you get home—even if
it's mid-afternoon. And don't spoil it by overcooking.*

BEVVY'S WELSHKAHN OYSTER PUFFA
(Oyster Corn Fritters)

You won't regret trying these with canned or fresh corn.

2 cups corn
2 eggs, separated
2 tablespoons flour
½ teaspoon salt
¼ teaspoon pepper

To the corn add the beaten egg yolks, flour, and seasonings. Add
the stiffly beaten egg whites and blend. Drop by spoonfuls the
size of an oyster on a hot, buttered frying pan, and brown gently
all around.

FRIED CORN

This has a nutty, delicate flavour and is easy to make. You can
use corn cut from the cobs after boiling for 5 minutes, or a can
of drained whole-kernel corn. Melt 2 or 3 tablespoons of **butter**
in a frying pan, add the **corn**, sprinkle it with **salt** and **pepper**
and a teaspoon of **sugar**, and let it fry slowly. Watch it as it
browns; it sticks easily.

CORN FRITTERS

I could make a whole meal of these doused with maple syrup.

1 cup flour
1 teaspoon baking powder
¾ teaspoon salt
2 eggs, beaten well
¼ cup milk
1½ cups corn, fresh, frozen, or canned
2 teaspoons melted shortening
Deep shortening for frying

Sift the flour, baking powder, and salt; combine the beaten eggs and milk and stir into the flour mixture. Add the corn and melted shortening. Drop tablespoonfuls into hot fat and watch them for 4 or 5 minutes till golden. Drain on brown paper. Eat hot.

CORN CHEESE FRITTERS

Add ½ cup grated cheese to the above recipe if you want a different taste thrill.

BAKED CORN CUSTARD

A loner can easily cut this recipe in half, but why not enjoy two meals of it? It's great with cold meat or bacon or with maple syrup!

Corn cut from 3 to 5 cobs, or about 2 cupfuls of
kernels, fresh, frozen, or niblets
1 cup milk
2 egg yolks, lightly beaten
2 tablespoons melted butter
1 tablespoon flour
1 tablespoon sugar
Salt and pepper
Pinch of curry powder (optional)
2 egg whites, beaten stiff

Stir everything but the egg whites together. Then beat the egg whites and fold them in. Pour all into a well-buttered baking dish and bake uncovered, at 350°F for about one hour, or until the custard is firm and golden brown.

CORN AND CHEESE CASSEROLE

This is a good and easy way to use leftover corn, or the corn you froze last fall.

About 2 cups corn kernels
2 eggs, beaten
1 cup milk
Salt and pepper
1 cup grated cheese
3 tablespoons minced onion

Topping:
2 tablespoons melted butter
½ cup dried breadcrumbs

Stir all but the topping together and pour into a well-buttered loaf pan or small casserole. Melt the butter, stir in the crumbs to absorb all the butter, and sprinkle over the corn mixture. Bake at 350°F for about 40 minutes. This is a great thing to put in a little broiler oven if you have one.

DRIED CORN

In Lancaster County, Pennsylvania, you can buy dried corn in packages; in Ontario you must make it yourself.

Cut the kernels from the cobs and spread them flat and thin on pans to dry in a 250°F oven; stir often to prevent them from burning or browning and to dry them evenly. When the kernels are hard as chicken feed, with no moisture left in them (or they'll become mouldy), put them in jars and store them in a dry place. They'll keep a long time but not forever. (I kept some I brought back from Lancaster. It became wormy and the winter birds on my patio loved it.)

CUCUMBERS

Delicate, tender, crisp, and watery, cucumbers are usually sliced thin and served raw. But, being related to zucchini, they can be cooked in the same way to make a pleasant, hot side dish. You don't have to peel them unless they are waxed.

Cucumber slices often appear in mixed salads or on a tray of crudités, but for me the best way—and truly delicious and refreshing—is a cucumber salad with a sour cream dressing or chilled cucumber vichyssoise soup, both described in Soups and Salads with Schmecks Appeal.

FRIED OR GRILLED CUCUMBERS

Even people who can't digest raw cucumbers seem to have no trouble with these. Peel—or don't peel—the **cucumbers** and cut them into ¼-inch slices. Proceed exactly as for fried eggplant (page 32). If you'd rather grill the breaded slices, put them side by side on a pan with a dot of **butter** on each slice and grill till golden, turn each slice over, dot again with butter, and grill till crisp.

BAKED CUCUMBERS

Delicate and delicious.

Peel **cucumbers** and cut in quarters lengthwise. Scoop out the seeds if they are large, sprinkle with **salt and pepper**. Put into a baking dish with dots of **butter** and bake at 350°F till the cucumbers are more or less transparent and soft. It doesn't take long. If you want to be a bit fancier, cut the cucumbers in half, scoop out the seeds, sprinkle with **salt**, and fill the cavities with a mixture of **breadcrumbs** and **grated cheese**, dot with bits of **butter**, and bake until clear.

BRITTANY FARMERS' MARKET

When I visited my friend Françoise in Brittany after she was married, we would go every Friday morning to the market in Concarneau. Françoise's cook, 80-year-old Jeanne, came with us and we all carried baskets to fill. The large town square at the end of the harbour was entirely occupied with makeshift tables and booths. Farmers from the countryside had brought in fresh lettuces, cheese, great mounds of strawberries, anemonies, brilliant blue iris, lilacs, onions, beets, shallots, potatoes, asparagus, everything colourful and gleaming. There were pies from Lacronan, golden breads in all shapes and sizes, croissants, pretty bunches of radishes with white tips and red tops.

We kept walking up and down the aisles where the food was displayed. Françoise would look over what she wanted to buy, pay for it, and put it into one of our baskets. And when they were all filled, we'd go back to the car and drive round the harbour through the narrow streets that led to her stone house on the edge of the sea. There we'd relax in the sun on the terrace until Jeanne called us to the dining room for lunch.

EGGPLANT

When I took the Stylish Entertainment Course at Rundles classy restaurant in Stratford, the chef du cuisine always called eggplant by its French name, "aubergine." I think it sounds so much nicer for this beautiful, shiny, purple, egg-shaped vegetable.

BROILED AUBERGINE

This is how Rundles' chef prepared eggplant.

1 tablespoon grated onion
½ teaspoon salt
2 cloves garlic, minced
¼ cup melted butter
1 medium aubergine

Blend the onion, salt, garlic, and butter. Cut the aubergine into ½-inch slices. Put them on a buttered baking sheet and brush with the seasoned butter. Broil about 5 inches from source of heat for about 5 minutes, basting once, then turning the slices carefully with a pancake turner and brushing with remaining butter mixture. Broil until tender—about 2 minutes longer—but watch them. Serve plain or with a tomato sauce. Or transfer the aubergine slices to a shallow baking dish, spread with a tomato sauce, and sprinkle generously with grated cheese. Or top each slice with a thin slice of tomato and cheese that will brown and bubble under the broiler. This is so good you might want to make it a whole meal.

FRIED EGGPLANT

One time at an exotic restaurant in Vancouver I had eggplant served in a slurpy sauce; it wasn't half as good as the way my mother made it; fried crisp and golden, the taste is divine.

1 eggplant
Salt
1 egg, beaten

1 tablespoon milk
Pepper
Fine breadcrumbs
Fat for frying

Peel off the beautiful purple skin of the eggplant and cut the remaining, denuded, now homely vegetable into slices less than ¼ of an inch thin. Dip each slice in egg mixed with milk and pepper, coat with breadcrumbs, and fry slowly in a little fat till the eggplant is tender inside the crisp crust. If you like, you can simply dip salted slices in flour, mixed with pepper, and fry them.

ENDIVE

BRAISED BELGIAN ENDIVE

I've never had Belgian endive in Canada except in a salad, but the most delicious way I've ever tasted it was in Paris, one evening, when I had dinner with a friend at his hotel. I wasn't given the recipe but I think this is the way it was done. It needs and deserves close attention.

> ¼ **cup butter or dripping from beef, pork, or bacon**
> **1 or 2 tablespoons brown sugar**
> ¼ **teaspoon basil**
> **4 heads Belgian endive**
> **Pepper**
> **1 cup consummé or broth from beef or pork**

Melt the butter in a heavy skillet over medium heat; sprinkle in the sugar and the dried basil. Arrange the endive in the skillet and sprinkle with pepper. Keep turning to brown all round. Add ¼ cup broth and simmer, uncovered, until the endive is tender, adding more broth as it's needed. It might take 30 minutes. By then the endive should have a golden-brown glaze.

I had this delicacy served on a hot plate with grilled pork chops, brown potatoes, and a side salad—thirty-six years ago—and I'll never forget it.

FIDDLEHEADS

Fiddleheads are not really a vegetable: they are the unopened leaves of a fern. When they first pop out of the wet ground in the spring they look like the heads of fiddles. You can buy them in frozen packages from New Brunswick, but they grow along streams all across Canada, and it is fun to put on rubber boots and look for them. Rose and Kent Murray have taken me with them to a secret place that they know and I mayn't tell where it is.

Only the little, round, curled-up tip of the fern should be taken and never more than a few from each plant or there will never be fiddleheads in that place again. Be sure you get the right fern and not one that might be bitter. (That might be a Murray secret, too.) The flavour of fiddleheads is mild, unlike anything else I can think of; it is also very nutritious.

When you get home, sit on your patio and blow or slough off the fluffy brown husks. Wash the heads well in lukewarm water, then soak in salted water to get rid of insects that like fiddleheads, too.

Cook the greens, uncovered, in a potful of salted water for about 7 minutes or until barely tender. Serve hot with butter, salt, and pepper. If you have too many to eat fresh you could freeze them for a special occasion.

GARLIC

BAKED GARLIC

At Rundles Restaurant in Stratford, where they always have unusual but fabulously delicious things on their menu, they once had baked garlic as an appetizer. I tried it: the outer covering was crisp and easily removed to get at the sweet, tender, delicate little buds. And you won't have to keep your hand self-consciously in front of your mouth when you go to the theatre after dinner.

EVA'S WAY

When Eva married Melvin, they went to live in a seven-bedroom, white brick house with an addition that was a self-contained living unit. "Such a big house for a young couple," I said, as Eva showed me around. "Why did you add more?"

"Well, you see, Melvin and I are taking over the farm from Eli and Lovina. They have no children so when they're old we'll look after them as if we were their children." She smiled happily. "The new part where they live is like a doddy house." (A doddy house is a grandfather house where parents retire when a young son takes over, the ideal way in which the Old Order Mennonites look after their aged and perpetuate their traditions.)

Whenever I stop my car at Eva's gate, she runs out to greet me with her welcoming smile. The bedrooms are occupied now by Joanna, Julia, Florence, Harvey, and little Eunice. Sometimes a hired man has a room, too. Eva and Melvin sleep in the bedroom downstairs. There is a bathroom now and another large addition for laundry, soap-making, maple syrup canning, and storage.

"Do you have time for a cup of tea?" Eva always asks me. She plugs in the kettle and puts on the table a dish of jamjams, cake, or a piece of pie she's just made. She rarely sits down to enjoy them with me; there's always something she must stir or take out of the oven—though she never makes me feel that her attention is divided.

Eva's kitchen has been modernized: pass-through cupboards divide the working area from the long table where meals are served. There is a dry sink at one end, a brown refrigerator and electric stove on one side, a big, shiny black cookstove on the other side, and under a window with plants blooming on the sill is a dough trough that Eva's pioneering forebears brought with them to Canada from Pennsylvania in 1801.

I don't know how Eva does it. Her big house is spotless and tidy, and she always looks radiant. She makes all her own clothes, and those of the children, and is ready to give Melvin a hand in the barn, the fields, or the sugarbush if he needs her. Morning and evening she milks twenty-one cows. Every day she cooks for at least seven people, very often sixteen. In the summer she picks fruit from the trees in her yard, hoes, weeds, and harvests the bountiful garden that runs along the lane bordered by well-tended roses, hollyhocks, marigolds, and Sweet William. She processes all the food that fills three large freezers, cans and preserves all the fruits, meats, and vegetables in hundreds of jars that stand on shelves from floor to ceiling along two basement walls.

Yet Eva always has time to be friendly, to read to the children, help her sister Hannah with picking and canning. She has time to make quilts, read books and the *National Geographic*, go to church and family gatherings, shop, and copy her favourite recipes for me to scatter throughout my cookbooks.

Of course, Eva, blissfully accepting the disciplines of the Old Order Mennonite sect, doesn't have the distraction of television, radio, or a car; with a black bonnet over her dainty prayer cap she rides briskly—but not many miles—in a shiny, black, open buggy behind one of Melvin's smartly groomed horses, come wind, rain, sunshine, or snow, and the awful danger of speeding cars on the highway.

GREENS

Greens—spinach, beet greens, swiss chard, and kale—are so good for you. Any of the greens can be used in the spinach recipes that follow. Wash greens in several waters—lukewarm at first, lifting the greens from each water so sand sinks to the bottom. Remove imperfect leaves and root ends. Boil in the water that clings to the leaves for 10 to 15 minutes—but don't let them get mushy. Drain. Season with butter, salt and pepper, or serve with lemon or vinegar, garnished with hard-boiled egg slices or bacon bits (or both), or buttered breadcrumbs.

CASSEROLE FOR GREENS

Here's a nice easy way of using spinach, beet greens, chard, or kale.

A lot of slightly chopped greens—a fairly large
   potful
2 cups sour cream
1 package dry onion soup mix
¼ cup grated cheese

Cook the greens in water clinging to the leaves (or about ¼ cup) for about 2 minutes. Drain well. Combine with the sour cream and onion soup mix. Put into a buttered casserole and sprinkle grated cheese over top. Bake in a 350°F oven for about 30 minutes.

CREAMED SPINACH WITH BACON

Keep fit: eat spinach. You won't feel like a martyr when it's made this way.

1 package fresh spinach—about 4 cups
2 slices bacon
1 onion, sliced
2 tablespoons flour
½ teaspoon salt
Pepper

1 clove garlic, minced
1 cup milk—or half sour cream

Cook the spinach. Drain well. Sauté the bacon and onion until bacon is crisp and onion is tender. Remove the pan from heat and stir in flour, salt, pepper, and garlic; blend well. Add the milk and cook, stirring, until sauce thickens. Stir in spinach and serve hot.

SUNFISH SPINACH (OR SWISS CHARD)

Occasionally my next door neighbour, Jack Kersell, brings me a big bag of Swiss chard from his garden. What to do with it? Chard can be used in any spinach recipe. This is my favourite because it's so easy and schmecksy. It's very good with almost any kind of meat and potatoes—especially chicken legs and sweet potatoes.

1 big bag of chard (or spinach), about 4 cups
1 or 2 tablespoons butter
1 onion, finely minced
1 tablespoon flour
½ to 1 cup sour cream
Salt and pepper

Carelessly cut the green part of the chard from the stems (if you use spinach you don't have to do this). Fill up your sink with water and dunk the leaves up and down until you think there is no more sand on them. Change the water two or three times if you're squeamish. Put the still-damp greens in a heavy pot. Cover with a lid and let the whole mass cook over moderate heat until soft. Drain well. (You can cool it and put it into a container in your freezer or fridge if you don't want to use it right away.) When you're ready, chop the cooked chard up a bit with a knife—you needn't be fussy.

Now melt the butter and cook the onion till soft. Blend in the flour, then add the sour cream. Cook over low heat, stirring until sightly thickened, then stir in the chard. Season with salt and pepper. Stir. Heat gently. (If you are having an oven dinner, you can heat it in the oven.)

SPINAT MIT BREE (Spinach with Broth)

You don't have that grim feeling about getting your vitamins
when you eat spinach like this.

4 cups spinach
2 tablespoons butter
1 teaspoon grated onion (optional)
2 tablespoons breadcrumbs
1 cup soup stock
Salt and pepper

Cook washed spinach until tender and press out excess water.
Heat the butter, add the onion, then the breadcrumbs and gradually the soup stock; let it thicken, then season with salt and
pepper. Add the hot drained spinach. Granish with hot, sliced,
hard-boiled eggs and bacon bits or, if you want a whole supper,
serve with a poached egg on top and toast underneath.

SPINACH IN A CHEESE SAUCE

Put cooked **spinach** into a **cheese sauce** and garnish with **buttered crumbs**. You won't know you're taking in iron.

JERUSALEM ARTICHOKES

*These knubbly, dark roots have absolutely no resemblance
to the beautiful, flowerlike artichokes that grow in the
fields of France and Italy, where they are an expensive
delicacy that can't be grown in Canada.*

*Unless you know someone who has a garden and grows
Jerusalem artichokes, you may have difficulty finding
them. I wouldn't bother looking for them myself, because I
don't think their appearance and bland flavour are worth
the effort, though they are rich in vitamins. They can be
used instead of potatoes, baked, boiled, or fried, and
served with seasonings and butter or a cream sauce.
Because they discolour quickly, they are best cooked in
their skins until they are tender. Test them with a
toothpick.*

*Bevvy Martin grows them and pickles them as she does
beets because her husband tells her he loves them.*

HELP FROM HANNAH AND EVA

One mild day in February I fetched Hannah and Eva to my house
to see the beautiful blooming pink and white amaryllis that had
been given to me at Christmas. We drank tea, ate cinnamon buns
I had made, and talked about cooking vegetables. I had asked
them to bring their handwritten cookbooks with them.

"I don't have many vegetable recipes in my book," Eva said.

"And I don't," Hannah said. "In the summer we just boil them
and eat them fresh from the garden, sometimes without even
butter."

"And in winter we just do whatever we think is good for
them," Eva said. "We don't need to follow a recipe—except for
a few." And they copied them out for me to put in this book.

KOHLRABI

Kohlrabi is an interesting, pale green, turnip-shaped bulb that grows just above the ground and has edible turnip-like leaves sprouting from the sides. But it tastes like cabbage. Thin raw slices can be used on a tray of crudités.

To cook, peel, cut into slices, and boil kohlrabi for at least 20 minutes, till tender. Serve with a cream or cheese sauce sprinkled with buttered crumbs or paprika.

Or season it with salt, pepper, and melted butter.

Or season with salt and pepper, marjoram and Parmesan cheese lightly mixed with it.

HANNAH'S KOHLRABI IN BROWN BUTTER SAUCE

"I've never grown kohlrabi in my garden," Hannah told me, "but I've eaten it at somebody else's place and asked for the recipe, so I must have liked it, though I can't really remember it."

2 kohlrabi
2 tablespoons flour
2 tablespoons butter
¾ cup cooking liquid and water
Salt and pepper

Peel kohlrabi, cut into bite-size pieces, and add a small amount of boiling, unsalted water. Boil until fork tender. Lightly brown flour in frying pan, stirring frequently. Add butter and stir constantly until thoroughly combined. Drain the kohlrabi, reserving liquid. Add enough cold water to make ¾ cup liquid. Slowly add liquid to flour mixture, stirring until sauce is smooth and thickened. Stir in the kohlrabi and season with salt and pepper.

LEEKS

Members of the onion family, leeks are used most often in soups and salads—more's the pity, because they have a sweet, delicate flavour when cooked and served with a main course. They should be cleaned under running water because soil collects between the layers. Trim away the dark green leaves, saving only the white solid parts. (Keep the leaves for soup.)

Leeks can be boiled or steamed for about 12 minutes, then drained and served with a cream, cheese, or tomato sauce, sprinkled with paprika. Best of all, follow the recipe for braised Belgian Endive (page 34) but don't cook the leeks nearly as long.

MUSHROOMS

I don't suppose mushrooms are considered a vegetable, but they are often blended with vegetables to give them flavour and class. They are delicious on their own.

Don't take chances on gathering and eating wild mushrooms unless you know for sure that they are safe. Mushroom poisoning is not a pleasant way to die. You really should know a lot about wild mushrooms; go to the nearest library and read, then find someone who knows mushrooms first hand.

My neighbour Belle knew shaggy manes and inkies; they grew sparsely in our lawns near the lake. We took turns gathering them so that every other day we could have a treat. On one of Belle's days she drank beer with friends, then felt her face flush and her hands tremble. One day after I had eaten my little feed of inkies I had lunch with friends in town and drank a daiquiri—one daiquiri. Wow! I felt as if I'd had six! There's something about inkies that makes it unsafe to drink alcohol within twenty-four hours.

Better stick to cultivated mushrooms—there are lots of them.

BUTTERED MUSHROOMS

My favourite way and the easiest is simply to sauté **mushrooms** in plenty of **butter**, seasoned with **salt** and **pepper**.

CREAMED MUSHROOMS

Sauté **mushrooms** in **butter**, sprinkle them with a tablespoon of **flour**, pour in about a cupful of heated **milk**, and stir until there is a cream sauce coating the mushrooms, then serve over buttered toast or English muffins.

A MUSHROOM MEAL

I think I could eat this whole thing at a sitting, but, being aware of my weight, of course I wouldn't. Oh, no.

1 pound fresh mushrooms
2 tablespoons flour
1 teaspoon salt
½ teaspoon pepper
3 tablespoons melted butter
¼ to ½ cup grated cheese
1 cup sour cream
1 tablespoon minced parsley

Clean the mushrooms and put them in a bag with the flour, salt, and pepper. Shake to coat well. Sauté the mushrooms in the butter for about 10 minutes. Add cheese and sour cream, stirring until the cheese is melted, but don't let the mixture boil. Serve over buttered toast or in patty shells, and sprinkle with parsley.

ONIONS

When I was very young I wouldn't eat onions. I said I didn't like them, though I probably hadn't even tasted them. If I found them in a salad or in anything where they were visible, I'd fish them out and put them on the edge of my plate.

Then, when I was a teenager, I was afraid onion breath would make me offensive and unkissable.

When I was living in a university residence, we were given ham, scalloped potatoes, and boiled onions with a cream sauce every Saturday night. If I didn't have a dinner date or enough money to go to a restaurant, I would stay in and eat that obnoxious meal—but I always refused onions.

Then one night in mid-term when I was gated for breaking house rules, a server put an onion on my plate. To my great and pleasant surprise I found out that onions were really quite good—even boiled onions in a cream sauce.

Now I put onions in many dishes. I feel deprived if I have to leave them out for friends who say they can't digest them.

BAKED ONIONS

Put onions in the oven in their skins and in about 30 minutes they will be completely soft, juicy, and mild, without any after effects. Perfect for loners with small broiler ovens.

BOILED ONIONS

With a cream or cheese sauce, boiled onions really are tasty.

ONIONS WITH CHEESE

Easy to do and delicious—especially with beef.

Skin some large **onions** and cut them into thick slices. Lay them on a buttered oven dish, spread them with soft **butter**, and bake them in the oven at 350°F till soft. Mix grated **cheese** with **salt, pepper**, and a little **mustard**; add enough **red wine** to make a thick paste. Spread the paste on the hot onions and put under the grill to brown the cheese.

CHEESE SCALLOPED ONIONS

This could be a main dish. With cheese, onions, and toast, it should warm your cockles.

3 large onions, sliced
1 cup grated Cheddar cheese
4 slices buttered toast, cut in ½-inch cubes
¼ cup butter
¼ cup flour
2 cups milk
½ teaspoon salt
Pepper
2 eggs, beaten

Cook the onions in boiling salted water for 10 to 15 minutes; drain, then put half the onions in a 2-quart casserole. Sprinkle on half the cheese, then half the toast cubes. Repeat onion and cheese layers. Melt butter, blend in flour, stir in milk gradually, and cook until thick, stirring all the time. Stir in salt, pepper, and eggs. Pour over onions, then top with remaining toast cubes. Bake at 350°F for 30 minutes.

TZVIVELLE PIE (Onion Pie)

Generations of Mennonites have served this, smothered with gravy, when they had a roast beef dinner.

> **Rich pastry to line a deep pie plate**
> **2 cups sliced onions**
> **3 tablespoons butter**
> **6 eggs, beaten**
> **1 cup milk**
> **Salt and pepper**

Gently fry the sliced onions in the butter till they are almost soft, then spread them over the pastry in the pie plate. Combine the beaten eggs, milk, and seasonings and pour the mixture over the onions. Bake the pie on the floor of the oven for 40 to 50 minutes at 350°F.

SHERRIED ONIONS

Here's something good to do with those big mild onions that you usually buy to slice on hamburgers in the back yard.

> **4 or 5 large onions, thickly sliced**
> **¼ cup butter**
> **1 teaspoon salt**
> **Pepper**
> **1 teaspoon sugar**
> **½ cup sherry**
> **¼ cup Parmesan cheese**

Now you have a choice: Either sauté the onions in the butter until tender, then sprinkle with the salt, pepper, and sugar, add the sherry, and heat but don't boil; sprinkle with Parmesan cheese and serve hot. Or put the onion slices into a buttered baking dish, sprinkle with salt, pepper, and sugar; cover and bake at 350°F for 30 minutes or until tender. Then pour in the sherry and sprinkle with Parmesan. Heat in the oven for a few minutes only. Serve hot.

PARSNIPS

This sweet-tasting, inexpensive vegetable is delicious with sausage or pork. Bevvy says she peels hers, cuts it in slices, and cooks it with a ham bone or in ham broth.

Sometimes she'll boil it in salted water and serve it with a cream sauce and buttered crumbs.

I like mine browned in the oven. I cut the parsnips into long slivers, boil them till they're almost tender; then I melt beef dripping or butter in a pan, stir the parsnips around in it, and put them into the oven till they're nicely browned, turning them occasionally. They come out slightly chewy, and people who have never liked parsnips ask me how it was done.

GLAZED PARSNIPS

Boil the parsnips until they are tender then finish them off as you would Belgian Endive (page 34).

Or you can arrange cooked parsnips in a casserole, sprinkling layers with ¼ cup **brown sugar**, **salt**, bits of **butter**, and **consommé** or broth. Bake at 350°F for about 30 minutes.

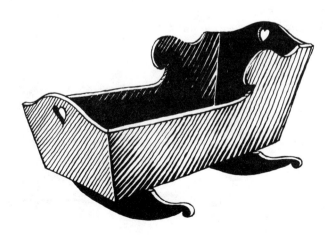

PEAS

*As soon as peas are ripe—in fact before they are ripe—I
go over to Hannah's place and ask for them. I can hardly
wait for that first fresh, sweet taste. I start taking them out
of the pods and eating them on my way home in my car.
And when I get home I sit in my sunny summer room and
keep eating raw peas until there aren't enough left to cook.*

FRESH GREEN PEAS

The most delicate, rare, and delicious vegetable of all. Peas need
to be boiled only a few minutes in salted water and served with
melted butter. I like to put fresh mint in the water as they're
cooking. If the peas are rather mature or frozen, I also add a
tablespoon of sugar to the cooking water.

SUGAR PEAS

These should be eaten fresh from the garden; they are hard
to find at the market and their season is very short—more's
the pity.

Cut off the stems, plunge the pods in boiling water until just
tender, not very long, drain them, and serve with lots of butter
melting over them and salt and pepper. Some people put bacon
bits over them, too, but why detract from that precious, delicate
flavour? This is a once-in-a-summertime thing.

PEPPERS

Sweet peppers or pimentos are usually not loners; they are most often mixed with other vegetables in casseroles, salads, soups, stir-fries, and relishes, or cut into strips and served on a tray with crudités. Because peppers don't keep long in the fridge, I buy them in season at the market, cut them into squares, and freeze them in small packages to be used in soups and casseroles whenever I need them. Norm and Ralph do the same. Ralph warns: "You have to be careful not to use too much. Cooked peppers have a strong flavour and can overpower everything else."

Norm and Ralph like peppers so well they often bake them as the vegetable with a main course. Norm cuts off the stem bit, slices them in half, cleans out the seeds and membranes, flavours the inside with salt and pepper, then drops a spoonful of butter into each half, and pops them into a 350°F oven for about half an hour, until soft.

Sometimes Norm puts thick vegetable soup into a whole pepper and bakes it.

Or she stuffs whole peppers with a mixture of cooked rice, sautéed onions, and bacon or ham. Sometimes she pours tomato soup over the peppers in the oven.

She also stuffs peppers with herbed bread and chopped meat or sausage stuffing. Norm is an inventive cook; she loves to experiment.

POTATO FILLING FOR PEPPERS

1 cup mashed potatoes (use leftovers)
1 egg, beaten
2 tablespoons butter
1 minced onion
1 tablespoon chopped parsley
¼ cup finely sliced celery
1 or 2 cups herb-flavoured dry bread cubes soaked
   in water then squeezed dry
6 green peppers, cored and seeded

Mix everything but the peppers together. Stuff the peppers, put a spoonful of butter on top of filling in each and bake at 350°F for 30 minutes.

CORN-STUFFED PEPPERS

Peppers and corn are in season at the same time; if you have a few cobs left over you could use them like this.

> 1 onion, chopped
> 2 tablespoons butter
> Cooked corn from several cobs—about 2 cups (or
>   canned corn or lima beans)
> Salt and pepper
> ½ cup milk, cream, or white sauce
> 4 or 5 green peppers
> Grated cheese or buttered breadcrumbs

Sauté the onion in butter until tender, then add the corn, seasonings, and milk. Stuff the peppers with the mixture and sprinkle with cheese or buttered crumbs or a blend of both. Place in a pan with just enough water to cover the bottom and bake at 350°F for about 30 minutes.

Try other stuffings—ham, hamburger, sausage meat mixed with bread cubes, eggs, onions. Do your own thing and be proud of yourself.

POTATOES

There seems to have been a conspiracy lately against home-cooked potatoes. I've heard women say, "They're so fattening," and they've served rice instead, though one medium baked potato has 95 calories; one cup of boiled rice has 200. For me no dinner is complete without potatoes; Bevvy cooks them three times a day.

I want a fair-sized serving with meat, gravy, and vegetables. It annoys me when I go to an expensive restaurant and I'm given two or three little barrel-shaped pieces of potato; I know the rest of a whole potato has been pared away into the garbage. My friend Françoise tells me that is how they serve potatoes in gourmet restaurants in Paris. So what? I don't want my potatoes to be fashionable and sparse; I want to have enough.

NOTES ON POTATOES

Mealy potatoes are best for baking, boiling, and frying—waxy ones for salads, scalloping, and creaming.

• Boil new potatoes in their skins.
• Shake potatoes over heat after they are drained to keep them dry.
• Don't let potatoes stand in water—they lose minerals and vitamins.

BAKED POTATOES

Best of all—but not wrapped in foil. Last year on a ride around Lake Superior every hotel dining room or restaurant gave us the usual choice of baked, mashed, or French fried potatoes. I always chose baked and invariably they came wrapped in foil: the skins were soft, scarred, and unappetizing, the potatoes were heavy, soggy, grey. Not till we reached the very special Flame Restaurant in Duluth were we given a treat: a baked potato that came to the table without foil. It had a crisp skin and a creamy, flaky interior; a dab of butter, salt, and freshly milled pepper made it a potato I'll never forget. I wish I could bake one as well.

I scrub my potatoes—preferably potatoes with a light, almost transparent skin; while the potato is wet I sprinkle it with salt, which sticks throughout the baking. To get the heat into the centre of the potato and to let the steam out I usually pierce the potato with an aluminum nail—to be pulled out after the potato is baked. I put the potatoes on a foil plate that can be shoved and squashed into a corner of the oven to make room for the roast—or whatever. I bake potatoes for 1 hour at 400°F or 1½ hours at 350°F, depending on the size and age—the young ones take longer. The more quickly they're done the better they'll be. Remove them from the oven, take out the nails, cut the skin on top to let the steam out, and serve immediately.

If you forget to put your potatoes into the oven soon enough to be ready on time—or if you're cooking something that doesn't take as long as it does to bake a potato—you can parboil them for a while first, then finish them in the oven—but don't expect that superb Duluth Flame texture and flavour.

STUFFED BAKED POTATOES

When Mother had company for dinner and meat without gravy, she often baked **potatoes** and stuffed them. She cut a slice off the top of each and carefully scooped out most of the inside; she mashed it and added **salt** and **pepper, butter** and a bit of **cream**. Then she stuffed the potatoes with the mixture, put a dab of butter and a sprinkling of **paprika** on each, and returned them to the oven to keep hot until serving.

POTATOES COQ D'OR

Kit's sister in England brought her this recipe—so simple and so good. People always ask how she did it.

Slice as many **potatoes** as you need very thinly. Reassemble the slices into potato shapes. Arrange them tightly in a buttered baking dish. This is not tricky, really, and you needn't be fussy. Sprinkle them with **salt, pepper,** and **onion flakes**. Add water to cover. Dot with **butter** or **margarine** and bake at 350°F for about 1½ hours. You'll be surprised.

WHOLE FRIED POTATOES

A rare treat one can have only in early summer when the first **new potatoes** come on the market. I always buy a basketful when I see them, marble-sized, more expensive than the larger ones, and with a flavour all their own. I boil them in their pale, clean, thin little jackets, turn them into a frying pan in which I have melted **butter**; I brown them, constantly stirring them around, sprinkle them with **salt** and **pepper** and, just before I serve them, I sprinkle a lot of **cut parsley** over them. Divine! Could anything be better? Yes—if you peel all the dear little potatoes after you've boiled them, as my patient, painstaking mother always did.

PAN-FRIED POTATOES

Bevvy serves fried potatoes at least once a day; always for breakfast with summer sausage, and often for supper with slices of leftover roast, an old-fashioned sausage, relish, pickled beets, and a sour cream salad of cucumbers, endive, or leafy green lettuce. "What could you have better?" she says. She'd be surprised to know there are people in the world who won't or don't know how to fry potatoes: "I never know what to do with leftover potatoes," they mutter as they throw the good vegetable into the garbage—while my thrifty soul cringes.

Beef dripping gives fried potatoes the best flavour, but you can use **lard** or **vegetable shortening** or **butter**—though butter burns quickly. Let the shortening melt and get hot in the frying pan before you put in your thinly sliced boiled or baked potatoes. Turn the heat down and let the potatoes brown slowly, turning them occasionally but not enough to make them mushy. Sprinkle them with **salt** and **pepper**—the seasoned variety if you like. Some people fry **onions** with potatoes; they should be fried till soft before putting the potatoes into the pan. If you use vegetable shortening as your fat, a bit of butter added before serving gives a better flavour. **Parsley, chives**, or **herbs** can be added as well.

If you don't have quite enough potatoes to go round, tear up slices of **buttered bread** to make up the amount you need and fry it along with the potatoes—it's almost an improvement.

RAW FRIED POTATOES

Quick, easy, and very, very good, a godsend if you haven't time
to boil or bake potatoes.

Use as many **potatoes** per person as you think will be eaten,
remembering that they shrink in the frying. If your potatoes are
thin-skinned, it is only necessary to scrub them. Slice them thin
on a slicer, then spread them in a frying pan where the **fat** is
almost sizzling. Turn down the heat, cover the pan, and let the
potatoes fry till they're golden brown and crisp on the bottom
and the mass of potatoes is soft when you prick it; with an egg
turner flip them over and brown on the other side without the
lid. If you have **summer sausage** to eat with these, so much the
better.

CREAMED POTATOES

I used to laboriously make a cream sauce and pour it over sliced
boiled potatoes; with parsley cut into them, they were very
good. But Bevvy has an easier way. She slices **raw potatoes**
into boiling, salted **water**—about 4 medium potatoes into 1 cup
of water—in a saucepan with a tight lid. When the potatoes are
soft—but not mushy—she adds ½ cup **cream**, or she pours off
half the water and adds 1 cup **milk** with 1 tablespoon **flour**
stirred into it. It takes only a few seconds to thicken. She adds
a good dollop of **butter**, then **parsley** or **chives**.

NEW POTATOES AND PEAS

Bevvy says this is a real summer dish—simple to make but with
that little bit extra.

> **4 good-sized new potatoes**
> **1 or 2 cups fresh peas**
> **½ teaspoon basil**
> **Pepper**
> **2 tablespoons butter**
> **2 well-rounded tablespoons sour cream**
> **Fresh cut-up parsley**

Scrub the potatoes and cut them in quarters. Put them into a saucepan with about ¾ inch of salted, boiling water. Cover and boil till almost done, then drop in the peas, and sprinkle in the basil; when the peas are soft enough to suit you, drain away any water that remains; add pepper, butter, and sour cream, and heat a few seconds. Turn into a serving dish and sprinkle with the fresh chopped parsley. Perfect with gravyless meat and a salad.

SCALLOPED POTATOES

Peel and slice **potatoes** fairly thin. Butter a baking dish, or a cake pan if you want to expose more surface so everyone at your table can hope to get some of the crusty brown top when Pappa is serving. Arrange some of the potato slices in the bottom of the baking dish, sprinkle them lightly with **flour, salt,** and **pepper**, and any other **flavours** or **herbs** you might like; dab on a few bits of **butter** and continue putting in layers of potatoes, et cetera, till you've used all the potatoes you've sliced. Now pour in enough **milk** to come not closer than an inch and a half from the top of your pan or it will boil over and be horribly smelly and messy. Put the potatoes into the oven at 300°F and leave them there for an hour and a half, or till they are soft with a golden crust.

POTATOES WITH A CHEESE SAUCE

Often when I have company from out of town where they can't get Kitchener's specialties, I like to serve smoked pork chops and with them potatoes that can be put in the oven and left there indefinitely till whatever hour my guests arrive, settle down, and have a drink or two.

I peel and boil in salted water as many medium-sized or cut-to-medium-sized **potatoes** as I'll need—usually two per person because they really make a hit. While the potatoes are boiling I make a medium thick, fairly rich, **whitesauce** (see page 84 and allow about ½ cup for each potato if you're the careful measuring type). To it I add chunks of **cheddar cheese** —about 1 cup for 6 potatoes. I put the hot, firm, boiled potatoes into a buttered casserole, pour the sauce over them, and pop them into the oven to keep warm at 200°F till my guests arrive. The top of the dish should be golden with streaks of brown.

I leave my potatoes on the bottom shelf of the oven while I'm grilling my smoked pork chops above them.

Warning: At no time during this process let the potatoes get cold.

CHEESE-SCALLOPED POTATOES AND CARROTS

Norm often makes this attractive dish for a buffet supper with cold meats and salad.

> **About 5 cups potatoes, pared and sliced thin**
> **5 carrots, sliced diagonally (about 2 cups)**
> **½ cup sliced onion**
>
> *Cheese sauce:*
> **3 tablespoons butter**
> **2 tablespoons flour**
> **1 teaspoon salt**
> **⅛ teaspoon pepper**
> **Dash of cayenne**
> **1½ cups milk, heated**
> **1½ cups grated Cheddar cheese**

Parboil the potatoes, carrots, and onion in salted, boiling water for 5 minutes. Drain. Make the cheese sauce: melt the butter, stir in the flour and seasonings, then the hot milk. Stir till it thickens, remove from the heat, and stir in half the cheese, leaving the rest for topping. In a buttered casserole, layer half the potatoes, onion, and carrots; top with half the cheese sauce; repeat with other half of vegetables and sauce. Sprinkle top with remaining cheese. Cover with foil and bake at 375°F for 30 minutes or until tender. Uncover top for last 10 minutes to brown. Sometimes Norm makes this in a large, deep Pyrex cake pan to expose more browned surface.

OVEN-GRILLED FRENCH FRIES

Because one can hardly avoid French fries when one eats out in a restaurant or a drive-in (and they are very well done), I never fry potatoes in deep fat. But I do occasionally make their equivalent in my oven.

After peeling and cutting the **potatoes** so they vaguely resemble French fries, I melt **beef dripping** or **vegetable shortening** on a large cookie sheet under my broiler. I pour the potatoes into the hot fat and turn them with an egg turner till they're all coated, then I put them under the broiler till they're golden brown, turn them over and brown them all around. By that time they should be soft in the middle and ready to eat—not saturated or soggy or impregnated with fat.

POTATOES BOILED IN THEIR JACKETS

When we were children, we had a maid at our house who, when our parents were out, used to boil **potatoes in their jackets**, peel them quickly, and give them to us hot, hot, in a soup dish with **warmed milk** and lots of **salt and pepper**. That's all she'd give us for our meal but we loved it; the potatoes had a really special flavour.

A BACHELOR'S DILEMMA

Sam Hatch leaned against the rail fence in Neil's Harbour and talked to me. "It seems t'rills is all the girls are looking for nowadays. I want more than that. I want clean shirts and square meals. I want someone to keep my house nice like my mother used to do—God rest her soul." Sam lowered his voice. "I'm 54 years old and I got a young girl who'd take me if I asked her to. She says, 'Sammie, you're sweet.' That's what she says. She's a fine, respectable girl. There's been nothing bad between us, no t'rills and grassing in the moonlight, nothing like that."

Sam closed his eyes for a second. "I don't know what to do about her. She wanted me to buy her a dress in the catalogue that cost ten dollars. I couldn't afford to keep a woman with such expensive taste as that." Sam rubbed his chin reflectively. "But the girl says, 'Sammie, you're sweet,' and that makes me feel young. She's 24. Maybe she's too young for me, it might be like gas and water, they don't mix. She might want nothing but sex and new dresses and I want socks without holes and mashed potatoes."

MASHED POTATOES

Need I tell you how? But some are so much better than others.

Peel your **potatoes**, cut them up into boiling, salted water and as soon as they're soft, pour off the water, mash the potatoes, and add **warmed milk** and **butter**; I can't tell you how much because I don't know how many potatoes you're using, but don't make the mixture too thin. (If you heat too much milk give it to the cat). Keep beating till the potatoes are creamy; lumps are unforgivable.

To keep them fluffy, add a bit of **baking powder**.

Serve at once. **Parsley** looks and tastes good whipped along with them.

CHEESE MASHED POTATOES

Mashed potatoes left over from your Sunday dinner? This is a fine way to use them next day with slices of cold meat.

> **2 to 3 cups mashed potatoes**
> **½ cup sour cream**
> **5 slices bacon, fried crisp**
> **3 onions, finely chopped**
> **1 cup grated Cheddar cheese**

Spread potatoes in a flat baking dish; smooth sour cream evenly over them. Crumble fried bacon and sprinkle over the sour cream. Sprinkle the onions over the bacon then cover with cheese. Bake in a 350°F oven for 30 minutes.

POTATO PATTIES

If you have **leftover mashed potatoes**, you can find all sorts of recipes to use them up, but the easiest way is to make potato patties. You can add a **slightly beaten egg** to the potatoes if you like or just take a good-sized heaping tablespoon of potatoes and with your hands shape it into a patty about ¾ of an inch thick. Coat it with **flour** or **fine breadcrumbs** and place carefully into a frying pan where you have melted and heated **dripping** or **butter**. Lower the heat and let the patties brown on one side, turn them over and brown on the other side. Very good.

POTATO SCONES

This is the best thing to do with leftover mashed potatoes. Combine half as much flour as you have leftover mashed potatoes—for example:

1 cup potatoes
½ cup flour
1 teaspoon baking powder
1 egg

Mix all together, bake on a griddle or in a frying pan in a bit of shortening or melted butter till they're golden and puffy; turn them over and brown the other side. They're delicious with meat or with butter and jam or syrup.

JILL'S POTATOES ROMANOFF

Really special to serve hot as a casserole or cold as potato salad.

6 large potatoes
4 cups sour cream
1½ cups shredded sharp Cheddar cheese
1 bunch green onions, sliced across stems
1½ teaspoons salts
¼ teaspoon pepper
Paprika

Cook the potatoes in their jackets until barely fork tender. Peel and slice or shred coarsely into a large bowl. Meanwhile, blend the sour cream, 1 cup of the cheese, the onions, salt, and pepper. Stir gently into the potatoes so you don't mush them. Put all into a buttered casserole, top with remaining cheese, and sprinkle with paprika. Cover and refrigerate several hours or overnight, or freeze for future use. Bake uncovered at 350°F for 30 to 40 minutes, till heated through—no longer.

HARVEST

Fall is the time of the year to rejoice. While the squirrels are gathering pine cones beside my cottage, I go to the farmers' market to glory in the bounty of the harvest: sweet cider, grapes that make wine, pumpkins, curly yellow endive, weirdly shaped gourds, everlasting straw flowers, purple plums, and shiny red apples. There are sure to be bargains where there is abundance. I run back and forth many times to my car with baskets of beets, parsnips, turnips, squash, apples, and red and green cabbages to store in my cool room for use in the winter. The squirrels with their pine cones have nothing on me.

HANNAH AND EVA'S POTATO PIE

"It's like a quiche," they told me, "but with a mashed-potato crust. Really easy and so good." Hannah added, "I just use whatever mashed potatoes are left over, combine with seasonings, and mix up the rest. It takes hardly any time to prepare."

> **6 medium potatoes**
> **1 teaspoon salt**
> **A few grains pepper**
> **1 teaspoon dry mustard**
> **1 tablespoon chopped parsley**
> **¼ cup chopped onion**
>
> *Filling:*
> **2 eggs, beaten**
> **1 cup grated cheese**
> **1 cup milk**
> **½ teaspoon salt**
> **Pepper**
> **¼ teaspoon rosemary**
> **1 tablespoon butter**

Mash the potatoes and stir in salt, pepper, mustard, parsley, and onion. Cover bottom and sides of a deep 10-inch pie plate or an 8 inch x 8 inch cake pan with potato mixture to form a crust. Combine eggs, cheese, milk, salt, pepper, and rosemary; pour into potato-lined pan. Dot with butter. Bake at 350°F for about 35 minutes or until golden.

SHERRIED SWEET POTATOES

This is not one of Bevvy's recipes. It came from the deep South—and tastes mighty good in the frozen North.

6 sweet potatoes, medium sized
¾ cup brown sugar
1½ tablespoons cornstarch
½ teaspoon salt
1½ cups orange juice
½ teaspoon grated orange rind
¼ cup raisins
4 tablespoons butter
¼ cup dry sherry
¼ cup pecans

Cook whole potatoes in boiling, salted water until tender. Peel and cut into ½-inch slices. Arrange in a flat baking dish—a 9 inch x 13 inch cake pan will do nicely. In a saucepan, combine brown sugar, cornstarch, salt, orange juice, rind, and raisins. Cook and stir over medium heat until bubbly and thickened. Add butter, sherry, and pecans, stirring until butter is melted. Pour over the potatoes and bake at 325°F for about 30 minutes, basting occasionally, until potatoes are well glazed.

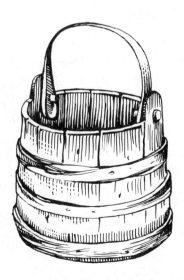

PUMPKIN

Don't buy a pumpkin just for Hallowe'en, but if you do make a jack-o'-lantern and it isn't smoked up, you can boil it and use it to make a pie or soufflé.

When my two sisters and I went on a tour of New Zealand we were often served a generous slice of buttered baked pumpkin as a vegetable with lamb and potatoes.

PUMPKIN SOUFFLÉ

This soufflé has an added touch: it can also be made with squash. Bake a 4- or 5-pound **pumpkin**, cut it in half, scoop out the seeds, then scrape out the pumpkin pulp and purée it.
Blend in 1 cup—more or less—**grated cheese**, 2 or 3 **eggs**, a generous dollop of **cream**—about ¼ cup—and **salt, pepper,** and a bit of **brown sugar**. Whip all this together, pour it into a buttered casserole dish, and bake it at 350°F until it rises and is set when you test it with a knife. It might take almost an hour—but watch it.

Pumpkin pies make the best use of pumpkin. There are several great recipes in *Pies and Tarts with Schmecks Appeal.*

SALSIFY

Scrape this long, spindly root, which looks like a small parsnip and tastes rather like oysters; slice it thin and cook it in salted water till tender. Dip pieces in a light **pancake batter** and fry to a golden brown, or serve it with a **white sauce** (page 84).

Or in a buttered baking dish, put a layer of cooked **salsify**, sprinkled with a few **celery seeds** and **parsley**, then a layer of **white sauce**. Alternate layers until the salsify is "all," as Bevvy would say. Top with **buttered breadcrumbs** and bake at 350°F for about 30 minutes.

BEVVY'S OYSTERS (SALSIFY)

With a horse and buggy it would take Bevvy's husband a long time to drive into town to buy a pint of oysters—and expensive, too. This is Bevvy's substitute. She grows salsify in her garden.

8 or 10 salsify
Salt and pepper
2 eggs, beaten
2 tablespoons lard or other shortening

Scrape and slice the salsify; boil in salted water until soft. Purée and season with salt and pepper; add beaten eggs. Heat the lard in a skillet and drop in spoonfuls of salsify mixture rounded to look like oysters. Brown on both sides and serve hot with ketchup.

SAUERKRAUT

I don't know why so many "superior" Anglo-Saxon types raise disparaging eyebrows at the mention of sauerkraut. They have probably never let themselves taste this easily digested, easily prepared delicacy that is a favourite in northern Europe and Waterloo County. It is simple and pure: nothing but shredded cabbage, salt, and boiling water. I've never made it: I think the sauerkraut that comes in cans is just dandy.

There seem to be several ways to prepare it, but all agree that the fresh cabbage should be shredded very finely and packed into glass jars or a stone crock. One recipe says: "Mix salt, enough to taste good, through the cabbage until it forms its own juice before you pack it tightly into quart jars." Bevvy says: "Stomp the cabbage down hard in a stone crock, keep adding and stomping until the crock is filled, sprinkling salt through the crock as you fill it, then add enough hot water to cover the cabbage." My friend Magdaline says: "Don't pack the cabbage tightly in the jars, just add a teaspoon of salt and fill the jar with boiling water." All agree that the jars should not be sealed tightly and should be put in a pan, as some of the juice will run out while the cabbage is fermenting—as it will do for several days. When the cabbage is no longer fermenting, remove the lid of the jar or crock, add enough cold water to fill the jar, and seal it tightly.

COOKING SAUERKRAUT

There are several ways: I've eaten it in Paris and Alsace boiled in white wine, in Germany cooked to a mush with onions and caraway seeds; I prefer it the Waterloo County way, which is "chenerally chust plain."

Most people boil it with a piece of **fresh pork** till the pork is tender. Often they put in some **dumplings** and boil the lot for 15 minutes more.

I bake my **sauerkraut** in a covered earthenware dish in the oven. I roast a piece of **pork** separately, then during the last hour of its roasting I put the dish of sauerkraut into the oven, adding 2 tablespoons of **brown sugar** and enough water to almost cover the kraut. When the meat is brown, I take it out of the pan, pour off the fat, turn the sauerkraut into the **brown meat drippings,** and stir it around till the brown dripping bits are all dissolved and absorbed. I pour the kraut back into the baking dish and carry it to the table where its wonderful warm aroma has lured everyone to wait with eager impatience as if they hadn't been fed for a month.

THAT SAUERKRAUT SMELL

I don't know any way that you can prevent the smell of cooking sauerkraut from permeating the house. Because it can be rather overpowering, I open the draft of my fireplace, light a bay-berry-scented candle, and occasionally open a door to let in a breeze. After a while I get used to the sauerkraut smell and let it take over, assuring myself that on a cold winter's day no aroma could be more warmly inviting.

SQUASH

You can have a great time if you try all the different kinds of squash, summer and winter. I like zucchini, but I don't find the other summer squashes worth bothering with: they are watery and haven't much flavour. The variety of winter squash is challenging: always easy to prepare, meaty, with a bright orange colour and distinctive flavour. They have thick skins and keep well for months in a cool, dry place.

Most often I use buttercup or turban, thin-skinned butternut, acorn, or pepper; if I need a lot I use a large, crinkly Hubbard.

To prepare, I simply wash the squash and put it on a foil plate that can be pushed into a corner of the oven when I'm cooking the rest of the dinner. I bake it for about an hour. When the squash is soft, cut it in half, scoop out the seeds (I give them to the birds), scoop the squash out of the shell into an oven dish, mash it, add salt and pepper, lots of butter, and enough cream or milk to make the mixture smooth like mashed potatoes. Sometimes I stir in a tablespoon of brown sugar. Then I put the dish into the oven until I'm ready to serve it. If there's any left over, I freeze it.

BAKED PEPPER SQUASH

If I want just enough squash for one or two eaters, I use pepper or acorn squash. Or I'll use two squash for four people. After washing the **squash**, I put it into the oven on a foil plate until it is almost tender. Then I take it from the oven, cut it in half or quarters, scoop out the seeds, drop a tablespoon of **butter** into each hollow, and season with **salt, pepper,** and a bit of **brown sugar**. Sometimes I'll put half a slice of **bacon** in each quarter. Back into the oven until the squash is tender and the bacon crisp.

SQUASH PUFF

Eva says, "Lovina sometimes makes this and, oh, it is so nice."

½ **cup chopped mild onion**
2 **tablespoons butter**
3 **cups cooked, mashed, or puréed squash (Hubbard,**
   butternut, or buttercup)
¼ **cup milk**
2 **large eggs, separated**
3 **tablespoons flour**
¼ **teaspoon salt**
1 **tablespoon baking powder**
⅛ **teaspoon pepper**
½ **cup buttered fine breadcrumbs (a must)**

In a large pan, sauté onions in butter until soft. Remove from heat and add mashed or puréed squash. Mix milk, egg yolks, flour, salt, baking powder, and pepper. Stir into squash. Beat egg whites until stiff. Fold in. Turn into ungreased straight-sided baking dish. Spread crumbs on top. Bake at 375°F for about 25 minutes or until puffy and golden.

Squash pies: Mother always used squash in pumpkin pie recipes, and they were wonderful. I can't resist telling you to find them in *Pies and Tarts with Schmecks Appeal.*

TOMATOES

*There is no better way to eat tomatoes than to get
home-grown ones in season, fresh from a garden; cut in
slices or wedges and sprinkled with salt and pepper. They
don't need a salad dressing or mayonnaise. My dad liked
to put them in a dish with sugar and vinegar.*

*As soon as tomatoes are ripe in the summer and until
they freeze in the fall, I eat tomatoes every single day. I
seldom cook tomatoes in summer; in winter I use frozen or
canned ones in stews, casseroles, and soups. And in case
you buy those anemic, tasteless, imported ones, I've given
you a few recipes that might give them some flavour.*

FROZEN TOMATOES

In the fall, when I'm afraid the tomatoes in the garden will soon
be frozen, I'd like to make them last forever. To keep them as
well as I can, I wash and dry some, put them on a tray, and freeze
them. Then I just let them find their way into the spaces among
the other frozen things. They look so perfect and beautiful and
are most handy to use when I need only one or two. I never thaw
them out before I use them because they become disappoint-
ingly mushy. But still useable.

LIZA GINGERICH'S CANNED TOMATO CASSEROLE

Every year—like all good Old Order Mennonites—Liza cans
jars and jars of tomatoes from her garden. This is her favourite
way of using them during the winter, all puffed up with a
buttery flavour. Really good.

> **6 or more slices of generously buttered bread**
> **1 quart canned tomatoes, or more**
> **1 mild onion, finely chopped**
> **1 teaspoon sugar**
> **Salt and pepper**
> **½ cup buttered breadcrumbs**

Put the buttered bread on a pan in a 200°F oven until it is thoroughly dry and crisp—but not brown, though that wouldn't hurt it. Cut or break each slice into four and lay half the pieces in the bottom of a well-buttered casserole. Pour in half the canned or frozen tomatoes; add half the onion and sugar, and sprinkle with salt and pepper. Cover with the rest of the bread squares, repeat the layers of tomato, onion, and seasonings. Spread buttered crumbs over all and bake at 300°F for 1½ hours. Bring it out puffy and amazingly tasty. You can prepare this in advance and refrigerate it until ready to bake.

SALEMA BAUMAN'S TOMATO PIE

This "pie" has no crust. Salema makes it when the tomatoes in her garden are ripe—or almost ripe. It is a good dish to make in winter when imported tomatoes have little flavour unless they are baked or grilled.

4 or 5 or more tomatoes, sliced thin
3 or 4 onions or more, sliced even thinner
1 or 2 cups breadcrumbs (you could use packaged
**   stuffing, finely ground)**
Salt and pepper
1 or 2 teaspoons sugar
1 teaspoon dried basil (if you don't use packaged
**   stuffing)**
¼ to ½ cup butter, fresh beef drippings, or bacon
**   fat**

Place alternate layers of tomatoes, onion, and breadcrumbs into a well-buttered pie plate or casserole, seasoning each layer with salt, pepper, sugar, and basil. On the top layer of breadcrumbs or on each layer, put very thin slices of butter or dripping. Bake in a 350°F oven until the top is nicely browned—about 45 minutes to 1 hour.

FRIED OR GRILLED TOMATOES

Firm slices of **red** or **green tomato** dipped in **flour** then **egg** and **crumbs** and fried in **butter**, or grilled, are easy to do and add colour and flavour to a plate. I like them with bacon and eggs for breakfast as I had them in England.

STEWED TOMATOES

A nice accompaniment for chops or fish.

   1 small onion, sliced or minced
   3 cups tomatoes—fresh or canned
   2 tablespoons butter
   ½ cup bread or biscuit crumbs
   1 tablespoon sugar
   Salt and pepper

Cook onions and tomatoes slowly till onions are tender—about 20 minutes, stirring occasionally. Add butter, breadcrumbs, sugar, and seasonings; cook a few minutes longer. Serve hot. Add cooked lima beans if you like.

STUFFED BAKED TOMATOES

Easy to do in the oven along with something else.

   6 large tomatoes
   1 cup breadcrumbs
   1 egg, well beaten
   2 tablespoons melted butter
   1 tablespoon minced onion
   1 teaspoon minced parsley
   ½ teaspoon salt
   Pepper
   A snippet of sage or savory

Cut out the centres of the tomatoes and stuff them with a combination of the rest of the ingredients listed. Put in a baking dish and bake at 350°F for about 30 minutes. Don't let the tomatoes get mushy.

SPINACH-CAPPED TOMATOES

You can make most of this the day before you serve it. It decorates a plate and it tastes good, too.

4 cups spinach or 2 packages frozen and thawed
1 minced onion
1 garlic glove, minced (optional)
¼ cup butter
1 cup breadcrumbs, herb flavoured
2 eggs, beaten
1 teaspoonn salt
4 large tomatoes cut in half

Cook the spinach about 5 minutes—until tender. Drain well. Cook the onion and garlic in the butter until tender, then add the drained spinach and stir together. Remove from heat and blend in the breadcrumbs, eggs, and salt. (Now, if you like, you can refrigerate this until next day.)

Place tomato halves, cut-side up, in a buttered 9 inch x 9 inch baking pan. Mound spinach mixture onto each tomato half, dividing the mixture evenly. Cover and refrigerate until an hour before you want to serve. (Or do the whole operation from the beginning without setting any of it aside.) Put the pan into a 350°F oven, uncovered, for about 35 minutes or until heated through. Lift each tomato carefully onto a plate to serve.

TURNIPS

For my Mennonite friends and my family, a turnip is the large, round, solid, heavy root that is pale orange throughout and has a purplish top on the outside. But according to the Canada Fresh Vegetable Regulation we are wrong: the proper name is rutabaga. A turnip is a much smaller, longish, white root with a more delicate flavour than that of the robust rutabaga—though recipes for cooking both are interchangeable.

In the stores the rutabaga is usually waxed to prevent dehydration. It must be peeled—and that is not easy to do. I put the turnip—pardon me, rutabaga—on a cutting board, place a long, heavy knife on top of it, and force it through the vegetable by pounding it with a hammer. I repeat the process (it gets easier as I get on with it) till the turnip is cut in half, then quarters, then eighths, and the slices are narrow enough to be peeled fairly easily. Then I cut it in chunks and boil it thoroughly.

I've never bought or eaten the small white turnips, so I can't tell you anything about them.

BOILED TURNIP

Bevvy and Mother always boiled **turnip** in **beef broth** and then added **butter**. You could also boil it thinly sliced, in salted water. Drain it, then mash it with **sour cream**, lots of **pepper**, and **parsley**.

MASHED TURNIPS

Turnip with turkey is a local tradition; the two flavours seem to complement each other. (Yellow turnips are stronger in flavour than white ones; to make them milder, combine with equal amounts of mashed potatoes.)

Peel and slice the **turnip** and boil it till tender in salted water. Drain, then mash or whip the turnip, add about ½ cup **butter** and plenty of **pepper**. Keep it hot in the oven till the bird is ready to be served. A garnish of **buttered breadcrumbs** and bits of **parsley** could do it no harm.

TURNIP AND APPLE CASSEROLE

Every year for Christmas dinner our extended family of 18 or 20 goes to the home of my niece Barbie and her husband, Peter; it's a big house on the hill with wonderful views of Wilmot Township in every direction. Each family unit shares in the preparation of the food, traditionally always the same: turkey, vegetables, cranberries, plum pudding, rum sauce, cookies, wine, and lemon snow. I am always delegated to bring the vegetables: mashed potatoes, peas, and turnip mashed with lots of butter.

One year I decided to give us a change; I'd found a recipe for a turnip casserole that I thought would be good. I made it; I liked it; but the family disagreed: they said it tasted all right but they preferred the plain mashed turnip that we've had every year of our lives. Amen.

For the family, I tripled this recipe. Try it on your immediate family or polite guests before you extend it.

    1 turnip
    1 teaspoon salt
    ¼ cup butter
    2 tablespoons brown sugar
    2 cups sliced apples

Cut the turnip in half, in quarters, then eighths; pare it—a helluva job—then cut it in chunks and boil it in just enough salted water to cover it. When it is soft, drain it thoroughly and add the butter and sugar as you mash it—or purée it in a food processor. Stir in the finely sliced apples and put it in a casserole and bake it at 400°F for about 30 minutes or until the apples are soft. Doesn't that sound good?

Good as Gold Soup, made with leftover turnip, is wonderful— see *Soups and Salads with Schmecks Appeal.*

ZUCCHINI

Zucchini is the most popular and prolific of the summer squashes; it grows madly, sprawling all over a garden if too many seeds are planted. It is especially delicate if caught and eaten when it is young, but most often it hides under its leaves and becomes long, fat, and overweight before it is discovered. Growers must be constantly alert : maturity comes to zucchini almost overnight.

One day I was at a ladies' luncheon, and, as we were leaving, one of the guests asked us to come to her car; she had a bushel of zucchini in the trunk and gave one or two to each of us. "I just can't keep up with them and I can't waste them," she told us.

Fortunately the bland flavour of zucchini blends well with other foods and gives moisture to vegetables, breads, muffins, and cakes. The skin and seeds are edible except in the big ones, which can be cut in half lengthwise and the seeds scooped out.

Zucchini can be eaten raw with a dip or in salads. Find as many ways to cook zucchini as you can—or invent ways. You're almost sure to be given one or two in August.

HERBY ZUCCHINI TOMATO CASSEROLE

A wonderful late summer dish that you can stretch or diminish to fit your largest or smallest casserole. A great way to use those overgrown zucchinis.

> 1 or 2 onions
> 2 tablespoons butter
> Enough zucchini, cut in ½-inch slices, to cover
>   your casserole
> 4 tomatoes, cut in ½-inch slices
> 1 teaspoon salt
> Pepper
> 1 garlic clove, squashed (optional)
> ½ teaspoon oregano
> 1 teaspoon basil

Topping:
1 cup grated Cheddar cheese
1 cup breadcrumbs
1 teaspoon blended herbs

Peel and slice an onion or two and cook long enough in the butter to soften it. Place the zucchini in the bottom of your casserole, put a slice of tomato on each slice of zucchini, sprinkle with softened onion, seasonings, and herbs. Put more zucchini slices, tomato slices, and well-seasoned onions until you have filled up the casserole. Cover and bake in a 300°F oven for about 20 minutes, until the zucchini is slightly tender. Take off the cover and bake another 10 minutes till some of the liquid has evaporated. Mix the cheese with the breadcrumbs and herbs, spread them over the top, and bake about 5 minutes longer until the cheese melts and the crumbs are a tempting golden brown. This is great with a tossed salad, baked potatoes, and country sausage, pork chops, lamb cutlets—any meat without gravy.

ZUCCHINI SAUTÉ

Nancy can whip this up in about five minutes; the tantalizing aroma of the garlic lasts longer.

1 medium zucchini
1 tablespoon oil
1 tablespoon butter
1 or more sliced onions
1 or 2 cloves garlic (optional)
1 or more tomatoes, cut in wedges

Cut the unpeeled zucchini in ½-inch slices. Heat the oil and butter at medium heat and cook the onion and garlic till soft; push to the sides of the pan. Drop in the zucchini so all the slices are in touch with the surface of the pan; cook till almost tender, then drop in the tomato wedges and let them simmer. Don't overcook the zucchini.

ZUCCHINI CASSEROLE

This very bland casserole is nice to have with or without meat.

4 eggs, beaten
¼ cup melted butter
1 teaspoon salt
¼ teaspoon pepper
2 tablespoons milk
2 cups unpeeled zucchini, grated in food processor
1 onion, finely chopped
1 cup grated Cheddar cheese
Pinch summer savoury and basil

Topping:
Grated cheese
Breadcrumbs

Blend the eggs, butter, seasonings, and milk, then add zucchini, onions, cheese, and herbs. Pour into a greased 1½-quart casserole and bake at 350°F for 25 minutes, or until the casserole is firm in the centre. It will puff up nicely and then go down again. About 5 minutes before it is ready to come out of the oven, sprinkle cheese and breadcrumbs over the top to brown.

MIXED VEGETABLES

Combinations of vegetables of various colours and textures can be most attractive, interesting, and flavoursome. Try whatever is in season and you can't go astray. The easiest way is to stir fry.

STIR-FRIED VEGETABLES

The best way to keep vitamins in tender, mixed vegetables. You don't need a wok though it is preferable; you can use a large heavy frying pan to cook vegetables in about 5 or 6 minutes. It takes much longer to prepare the vegetables because they should be more or less uniform in size. Those that take longer to cook are put in first, and the tender, moist ones are added later so they are all done at the same time.

Use any vegetables that you'd serve crisp-tender—none that need to be well cooked and mashed like potatoes, turnip, winter squash, or beets.

Put oil into your wok—2 teaspoons to a pound of vegetables—and place it over medium-high heat. When you can smell it, drop in the vegetables that are hardest and thickest: cauliflower and broccoli flowerets, Brussel sprouts, wax beans, sliced carrots, onions, minced garlic. I'm not suggesting that you use all of these—just what you happen to have or what appeals to you. Stir fry for 2 or 3 minutes then add pepper strips, celery, cabbage, zucchini slices, or anything similar; stir fry all together for another minute or two. Corn or peas in season? Drop them in. Now cover, turn heat to low, and let the vegetables steam for a couple of minutes, then uncover and stir in tomato wedges—if you want them—dried or finely chopped fresh herbs, salt, pepper, and a bit of sugar to taste.

Call your diners to the table and serve fast.

AUGUST MEDLEY

Make this in late summer when all the vegetables are fresh and wonderful and abundant. Combine any vegetables you like but especially:

> **1 pound green beans, sliced diagonally**
> **1 cup sliced green or red pepper**
> **1 pound slivered carrots**
> **2 onions, finely sliced**
> **2 or 3 tomatoes, cut in quarters**
> **1½ cups little mushrooms**
> **¼ cup fresh lima beans**

Mix together and place in a buttered casserole dish. Melt and pour over the vegetables:

> **½ cup butter**
> **1 tablespoon of your favourite herb or a mixture of several**
> **1 teaspoon salt**
> **Pepper**

Bake, covered, at 350°F for about 1 hour or stir fry, putting the tomatoes in after the other vegetables have softened.

EVA'S HARVEST CASSEROLE

This Mennonite dish can be made with squash, turnip, pumpkin, or overlarge zucchini. I forgot the eggs on the day I made it with turnip, but Norm liked it so well she asked for the recipe so she could serve it to her luncheon bridge with cold ham and red cabbage and beet salad.

> **2½ cups diced squash or turnip or pumpkin or zucchini**
> **1 cup sliced celery**
> **1 cup sliced onion**
> **A lump of butter as large as you like**
> **1½ cups water**
> **2 eggs**

Salt and pepper
1 cup bread or cracker crumbs
1 cup grated cheese
A sprinkling of wheat germ

Boil the squash, celery, onion, butter, and water for 5 minutes. Drain. Stir in eggs, salt, pepper, and half the crumbs and cheese. Top with remaining crumbs and cheese and wheat germ. Bake at 350°F for 30 to 35 minutes, adding water if needed.

VEGETABLE RICE

It's amazing what one can do with a cupful or two of cooked rice. In no time at all you can have an almost complete meal for one or two.

1 onion, finely sliced
2 tablespoons cooking oil
1 large carrot, finely sliced
1 stalk celery, finely sliced
1 tomato, finely chopped
Salt and pepper
1 to 2 tablespoons soy sauce or 1 teaspoon mixed
**   herbs**
2 cups cooked rice

Cook the onion in the oil until it is soft. Add the carrot, celery, and tomato, and cook slowly until the vegetables are almost soft. Sprinkle with salt and pepper and herbs or soy sauce. Add the rice, stir, put a lid on the saucepan, and keep it on moderate heat until everything is heated through. Serve it with cold meat or whatever you have that wants eating.

RATATOUILLE AUX PARMESAN

An impressive, colourful, French vegetable casserole that can be made the day before serving, hot or cold. John Walker, chef at Rundles in Stratford, performed this for us, and we thought it was wonderful.

½ cup olive or corn oil
2 onions, sliced not too fine
2 green peppers, roughly cubed
Salt and black pepper
2 aubergines (eggplant), cubed or sliced
2 courgettes (small zucchini), cut into ½-inch slices
2 large garlic cloves, crushed
Pinch oregano
Pinch basil or thyme
4 or 6 tomatoes, peeled, seeded, and chopped
½ cup grated Parmesan cheese
1 tablespoon chopped parsley

John told us this is a peasant dish. You should be able to see the form of the vegetables; if they're cut too fine they'll cook into a mush. Remember that.

Heat the olive oil, add the onions, and sauté lightly, add the green peppers and sauté them lightly as well, turning them over. Don't cook them. Season with salt and pepper. With a slotted spoon remove to a casserole. In the oil, sauté the egg-plant and zucchini with the well-squashed garlic; season lightly with the herbs. Zucchini and eggplant take lots of seasoning because they don't have much flavour of their own. Don't *cook* them in the oil, just lightly sauté them; shake the pan. Place in the casserole with the onions and peppers, add the tomatoes, and simmer gently, covered, for 30 minutes, or put in a 350°F oven for half an hour, well covered. Stir, but not often, or you'll muck it up. The vegetables really stew in the oil; the only actual liquid they have is from the tomatoes. The amount drops quite a lot as it cooks. Now uncover the dish and cook for about 10 minutes before serving; sprinkle with Parmesan and brown under the grill, then sprinkle over top the chopped parsley and enjoy the complimentary remarks you'll hear.

SIDE-DISH VEGETABLES

Must vegetables be the also-ran part of a meal? Trying to re-member the vegetables in my life that were outstanding, I recall those I've been thrilled with in France where they were served with subtle, mysterious sauces; those in good Chinese restau-rants where they were cooked very little; some in friends' homes; or at Rundles Restaurant in Stratford. Only at Mother's and Bevvy's tables, where the vegetables were flavoured with meat broths, sprinkled with butter-browned crumbs, or stirred into a sour cream dressing, have I heaped up second helpings— or thirds.

SAUCES FOR VEGETABLES

WHITE (OR CREAM) SAUCE

In case you need reminding how to make this:

2 tablespoons butter
2 tablespoons flour
1 cup milk
Salt and pepper

Melt the butter, add the flour, and stir until blended. Slowly add the milk and cook until the mixture thickens, stirring constantly. Add seasonings.

CHEESE SAUCE

Make a white sauce and in it melt ¼ to ½ cup cut-up or grated cheese. Stir till smooth.

BROWN SAUCE

Has more flavour than plain white sauce.

2 tablespoons butter or beef drippings
2 tablespoons flour
1 cup meat or vegetable stock
Salt and pepper

Melt the butter or drippings (and, if you like, add a small chopped onion). Carefully let the butter brown, add the flour, and stir till it, too, is brown. Add the liquid gradually, stirring constantly. Cook until thickened. Season with salt and pepper.

This should be timed so you can use the water in which your vegetable has been cooking. Or you might use a combination of vegetable stocks. Or you might add a teaspoon of meat broth base, or a bouillon cube. Or use meat stock instead of vegetable stock. Taste it, then pour it over your vegetables.

You can use this sauce over hot meats, dumplings, noodles, et cetera. It's especially nice over vegetables when you're having steak or chops, or meat that hasn't any gravy of its own.

PARSLEY SAUCE

Put lots of very finely chopped fresh **parsley** in **white sauce** and pour it over cooked, sliced carrots, green beans that have gone limp, cauliflower—or whatever you think it might be good for.

CURRY SAUCE

Sometimes a bit of **curry powder** in a **white** or **brown sauce** will send a vegetable to stardom. Use your discretion.

HERB SAUCE

Add some **herbs**—about 1 teaspoon to 1 cup of **sauce**, white or brown.

EGG SAUCE

Add coarsely chopped hard-boiled **eggs** to a **white sauce** for cooked asparagus or green beans.

HORSERADISH SAUCE

A bit of horseradish added to a sauce made with vegetable stock would give a nip to an ailing vegetable—but don't serve it to me.

BLENDED HOLLANDAISE SAUCE

I won't give you the slow method—look it up in another book if you want it. This is so easy.

Simply melt ¼ cup butter to bubbling—not brown.

Into your electric blender put

3 egg yolks
½ teaspoon salt
A sprinkle of cayenne
2 tablespoons lemon juice

Turn motor on and off, then turn it to low speed, and add the hot butter gradually in a steady stream. Blend about 10 seconds, or until the sauce is thickened and smooth. Turn off the motor. Keep the sauce warm in a double boiler or cool and refrigerate it, then reheat when you need it, adding 1 or 2 tablespoons of hot water or more lemon juice if you think it's too thick.

BUTTERED CRUMBS

Eva, Hannah, Bevvy, and I sprinkle them over all vegetables with a sauce and over some that are merely buttered.

Melt and brown 2 tablespoons **butter** in a pan; add ¼ cup fine **breadcrumbs**, and brown them in the butter, stirring all the time.

BOUQUET GARNI

If some of your vegetables are a bit tired, you could always put a bouquet garni in the water when you boil them. During the Stylish Entertainment course at Rundles Restaurant in Stratford, John Walker, the chef du cuisine, would often say, "Drop in a bouquet garni." He told us to keep a small supply on hand to use to pep up soup, stock, a sauce, or boiled vegetables.

Cut cheesecloth or muslin into 3- or 4-inch squares and in each one put whatever herbs you like; tie up the cloth with string so the herbs won't escape, and store the bags in a tight jar. Don't make too many at a time: the fresher they are the better. You can vary the flavours: dried parsley or celery leaves, thyme, bay leaf, chives, tarragon, chervil, garlic, fennel, marjoram, basil, sage, rosemary, et cetera.

HERBS WITH VEGETABLES

Fresh or dried herbs cooked with or sprinkled over vegetables give them a lift—especially in winter.

Asparagus: I wouldn't adulterate it.

Beans, green or yellow wax: basil, marjoram, thyme, dill

Limas or dried: savory, chili, or curry powder, dill, sage, or rosemary

Beets: basil, savory, allspice, dill, or ginger

Broccoli: dill, marjoram, rosemary, tarragon

Brussel sprouts: dill, marjoram, mustard

Carrots: basil, savory, thyme, or mint, dill, ginger, sage, or curry powder

Cauliflower: celery seed, dill, tarragon, nutmeg

Cabbage: mint, garlic, basil, savory, thyme

Corn: curry, oregano

Kale: oregano, marjoram

Kohlrabi: marjoram

Onions: bay leaves, curry, sage, thyme

Peas: mint, basil, savory, thyme, tarragon—but only if peas are old or frozen

Potatoes: parsley, chives, some herbs—but don't mess around

Squash: basil, oregano, thyme, bay leaves, tarragon

Sweet potatoes: cinnamon, cloves, nutmeg

Turnips: dill, sage

Tomatoes: basil, sage, tarragon

Zucchini: dill, sage—zucchini will take almost anything.

I haven't tried all these combinations—I copied them from various books, and all of them didn't agree. You have to experiment and use what you like. Remember not to overdo the herbs: you don't need to disguise the flavour of the vegetables.

BLENDED BUTTERS

If you want to enhance the flavour of vegetables, you might blend herbs with butter and stir the mixture with hot vegetables. Or you could keep the blended butter in your fridge until you are ready to use it. These ideas were suggested to us by the chef of the Stylish Entertainment course at Rundles restaurant.

HERB BUTTER

Most popular.

> **⅔ cup soft butter**
> **2 teaspoons lemon juice**
> **1 or 2 tablespoons finely chopped fresh herbs—use**
> **less if using dried herbs**
> **Salt and pepper**

Blend the butter and lemon juice, add the herbs and seasonings, beat until smooth. Very simple.

PARSLEY OR CHIVE BUTTER

Try it with carrots, potatoes, cauliflower. Substitute fresh dill.

> **⅔ cup softened butter**
> **1 or 2 tablespoons lemon juice**
> **2 tablespoons finely chopped chives or parsley**
> **Salt and pepper**

Blend well with a fork. Heap in a serving dish or mix with hot vegetables.

CURRY BUTTER

Nice with carrots, lima beans or onions.

> **½ cup softened butter**
> **½ teaspoon curry powder**
> **Salt and pepper**

Combine and beat until well blended.

GARLIC BUTTER

If you think some of your eaters don't like garlic, put this in a serving dish and pass it around the table. Most vegetables won't take it, either.

½ cup softened butter
2 or 3 cloves garlic, very finely minced
Salt and pepper

Combine and beat with a fork. Use on garlic bread or meats.

INDEX

Asparagus
  casserole, 5
  French, 5
  fromage, 6
  keeping and freezing, 4
  springtime, 4
  water for soups and drinks, 4

Beans
  baked, 11
  canned, 12
  canned bean recipe, 9
  Caribbean baked, 11
  dried, 10
  limas in cream, 12
  herbed and buttered limas, 12
  in August medley, 80
  schnippled bean salad, 8
  schnitzel, 10
  Swiss bean or carrot
    casserole, 8
  with herbs, nuts, onion,
    chives, parsley, sauces,
    sour cream, or mushrooms, 7
Beets
  greens, 38
  sweet and sour, 13
Blended Butters
  chive, 88
  curry, 88
  garlic, 89
  herb, 88
  parsley, 88
Broccoli
  casserole, 15
  divan, 16
  lemon dressing for, 17
  snow-capped, 14
  stir-fried, 79
Brussels Sprouts
  savoury, 17
  stir-fried, 79

Cabbage
  bubble and squeak, 20

Chinese, 19
  hot slaw, 18
  red, 20
  stir-fried, 79
  with cheese, 19
Carrots
  baked, 21
  casserole, 22
  glazed, 22
  in August medley, 80
  loaf, 23
  and onions, 21
  stir-fried, 79
  Swiss bean or carrot
    casserole, 8
  tired, 23
  with vegetable rice, 81
Cauliflower
  see Broccoli recipes, 14-17
  crudités, 25
  stir-fried, 79
Celery
  in harvest casserole, 80
  stir-fried, 79
  with crudités, sauces,
    nuts, 26
Celeriac, 26
Chard, 39
Corn
  baked corn custard, 28
  and cheese casserole, 29
  dried, 29
  fried, 27
  fritters, 28
    corn and cheese, 28
    oyster corn, 27
  stir-fried, 79
Cucumbers
  baked, 30
  fried or grilled, 30

Eggplant
  broiled, 32
  fried, 32
  in ratatouille, 82

Endive
  braised Belgian, 34

Fiddleheads, 35

Garlic
  baked, 36
  in ratatouille, 82
  stir-fried, 79
Greens
  beet, chard, kale, spinach, 38
  casserole, 38

Herbs with Vegetables, 87

Jerusalem Artichokes
  baked, fried, or pickled, 41

Kohlrabi
  in brown butter sauce, 42

Leeks
  see also Belgian endive, 34
  in cheese, cream, or tomato
    sauce, 43

Mixed Vegetables
  August medley, 80
  harvest casserole, 80
  ratatouille, 82
  side-dish, 83
  stir-fried, 79
  vegetable rice, 81
Mushrooms
  buttered or creamed, 44
  in August medley, 80
  mushroom meal, 45
  shaggy manes and
    inkeys, 44

Onions
  baked or boiled, 46
  in August medley, 80
    harvest casserole, 80
    ratatouille, 82
    vegetable rice, 81
  pie, 48
  scalloped, 47
  sherried, 48

  stir-fried, 79
  with cheese, 47

Parsnips
  casserole, 49
  glazed, 49
  oven-browned, 49
Peas
  fresh, with mint, 50
  stir-fried, 79
  sugar, 50
Peppers
  baked, 51
  corn-stuffed, 52
  freezing, 51
  in August medley, 80
    ratatouille, 82
  potato-filled, 51
  stir-fried, 79
  stuffed, 51
Potatoes
  baked, 53
  boiled in jackets, 59
  coq d'or, 54
  creamed, 56
  fried
    pan, 55
    oven-grilled French, 58
    raw, 56
    whole, 55
  in harvest casserole, 80
  mashed, 60
    with cheese, 60
  new, with peas, 56
  patties, 60
  pie, 62
  Romanoff, 61
  scones, 61
  scalloped, 57
    with cheese and carrots, 58
  sherried sweet, 63
  stuffed, 54
  with cheese sauce, 57
Pumpkin
  in harvest casserole, 80
  pie, 64
  soufflé, 64

Rutabagas (*see* Turnips, 74)

Salsify
  casserole, 65
  in pancake batter, 65
  oysters, 65
Sauces for Vegetables
  bouquet garni, 86
  brown, 84
  buttered crumbs, 86
  cheese, 84
  cream, 84
  curry, 85
  egg, 85
  herb, 85
  hollandaise, 86
  horseradish, 85
  parsley, 85
  white, 84
Sauerkraut
  baked, 66
  in white wine, 66
  smell, 67
  with fresh pork and
    dumplings, 66
Spinach
  creamed with bacon, 38
  in a cheese sauce, 40
  sunfish (chard), 39
  with broth, 39
Squash
  baked pepper, 68

  in harvest casserole, 80
  pies, 69
  puff, 69

Tomatoes
  canned tomato
    casserole, 70
  fried or grilled, 72
  frozen, 70
  in August medley, 80
    ratatouille, 82
    vegetable rice, 81
  pie, 71
  spinach-capped, 73
  stewed, 72
  stuffed, 72
Turnips
  and apple casserole, 75
  boiled, 74
  mashed, 74
  soup, 75

Zucchini
  casserole, 78
  herby, tomato
    casserole, 76
  in harvest casserole, 80
    ratatouille, 82
  sauté, 77
  stir-fried, 79